Let's Get Social

The Educator's Guide to Edmodo

Ginger Carlson and Raphael Raphael

International Society for Technology in Education
EUGENE, OREGON • ARLINGTON, VIRGINIA

Let's Get Social
The Educator's Guide to Edmodo
Ginger Carlson and Raphael Raphael

Editor: *Emily Reed*
Copy Editor: *Kristin Landon*
Proofreader: *Ann Skaugset*
Indexer: *Terri Morrissey*
Book Design and Production: *Kim McGovern*
Cover Design: *Brianne Beigh*

Library of Congress Cataloging-in-Publication Data

Carlson, Ginger (Ginger L.), 1973-
    Let's get social : the educator's guide to Edmodo / Ginger Carlson and Raphael Raphael.
      pages cm
    Includes bibliographical references and index.
    ISBN 978-1-56484-356-2 (pbk.) — ISBN 978-1-56484-499-6 (ebook)
    1. Edmodo (Electronic resource) 2. Education—Computer network resources.
  3. Internet in education. 4. Online social networks. 5. Teachers—Social networks.
  6. Students—Social networks.   I. Raphael, Raphael. II. Title.
    LB1044.87.C36 2015
    371.33'44678—dc23

                                                                                    2014048567

First Edition
ISBN: 978-1-56484-356-2 (paperback)
ISBN: 978-1-56484-499-6 (e-book)

Printed in the United States of America

ISTE® is a registered trademark of the International Society for Technology in Education.

About ISTE

The International Society for Technology in Education (ISTE) is the premier nonprofit organization serving educators and education leaders committed to empowering connected learners in a connected world. ISTE serves more than 100,000 education stakeholders throughout the world.

ISTE's innovative offerings include the ISTE Conference & Expo, one of the biggest, most comprehensive ed tech events in the world—as well as the widely adopted ISTE Standards for learning, teaching and leading in the digital age and a robust suite of professional learning resources, including webinars, online courses, consulting services for schools and districts, books, and peer-reviewed journals and publications. Visit iste.org to learn more.

Also by the Authors

By Ginger Carlson

Child of Wonder: Nurturing Creative and Naturally Curious Children (Common Ground Press, 2008)

Just Add Wonder: Cooking Activities to Nurture and Nourish the Creative Child (Common Ground Press, 2015)

Adventures in Gentle Discipline, featured essayist (La Leche League International, 2004)

By Raphael Raphael

Transnational Stardom, co-editor (Palgrave Macmillan, 2013)

DIS/Art: The Journal of Disability Culture and Visual Art, co-Editor

Research in Disability Studies: International Journal, Associate Editor

Teaching Film, Contributing writer (Modern Language Association, 2012)

About the Authors

Ginger Carlson has over 20 years of experience working with schools, families, and educational organizations around the world. Ginger has written and presented widely on the topics of Instructional Technology and Creativity and how to nurture them in our homes and schools. She is the author of *Child of Wonder: Nurturing Creative and Naturally Curious Children* and the subsequent book in the series, *Just Add Wonder: Cooking Activities to Nurture and Nourish the Creative Child.* Ms. Carlson holds a Master of Arts in Education and Instructional Technology from Pepperdine University and is a graduate of the Education Administration and Supervision Johns Hopkins University & ISTE program. She is currently serving as a member of the administrative team at the American Community School of Athens in Athens, Greece.

Dr. Raphael Raphael has been an educator in various capacities for the past 20 years, both in the United States and in international schools in Asia, Europe, and Eurasia. He has served in PK–12 and university settings. Dr. Raphael is an advocate for media education, and his writings on media literacy and education appear in numerous books and publications, including works by Modern Language Association, ISTE, and in the book *Transnational Stardom*, co-edited with Russell Meuff (Palgrave Macmillan, 2013.) He is also Associate Editor for the journal *Review of Disability Studies* and the co-editor of *DIS/ART: The Journal of Disability Culture and the Visual Arts.* Dr. Raphael also lectures for the College of Education for the University of Hawaii at Manoa and works as Technology Coach and faculty in international school settings. Dr. Raphael holds a Masters in Instructional Technology and Media Development from Teachers College Columbia University in New York City and a Ph.D. in English (structured emphasis in Film Studies) from the University of Oregon, in Eugene, Oregon. His writing and media teaching are also informed by his own work as a digital film and media artist.

Together, Dr. Raphael and Ms. Carlson lead the *Institute for Playful Learning*, (ifplay.org) a global organization that advocates for playful engagement in learning.

Acknowledgments

We wish to thank a few special people who were instrumental in bringing this book to life: Anita McNear at ISTE for her initial enthusiasm about the idea for this book; Frank Eastham at Johns Hopkins University for his support throughout the early process; Lynda Gansel at ISTE for her feedback in making this book as valuable a resource as possible; and Emily Reed at ISTE for her careful feedback and invaluable guidance in helping us to shape this book.

We would also like to thank all of our colleagues in the Edmodo extended learning community whose lively and enthusiastic digital presence inform this work, some through direct quotations, and many more who have inspired us with their enthusiastic and generous participation. In particular, we wish to thank the following educators for lending their voices in the "Tales from the Trail" segments in the Edmodo Toolkit: Cristina Betancourt, Lawrence J. Burns, Tawny Callaghan, Christina Cagliostro, Mrs. Cisneros, Timonious Downing, Joelle Dulaney, Tracy Feighery, Shauna Geary, Wendy Heyd, Kristina Holzweiss, Amanda Kerschen, Karen Kretschmann, Corazon Libao, Robert Maw, Erin Montgomery, Ann Marie Palmer, Kari Salomon, Kerrie Swepston, Jo Stone, Naomi Rodriguez Timmons, Kerry Townsend, Nick McWhirter, Vanita Vance, and Kelly Vazquez.

Dedication

For Anjali and Zeal,
and the world they will help create!
R. and G.

Contents

Chapter 8
Making Connections with Edmodo

Appendix A
Glossary

Appendix B
ISTE Standards

Appendix C
References

Introduction

Certain ideas can be used as tools to think with over a lifetime.

–Seymour Papert, Mindstorms: Children, Computers and Powerful Ideas

There is no tool like a tool whose time has come. Those of us interested in technology and education stand at a unique moment in history, where many of the original dreams about the ways technology could be used as a tool to transform classrooms, education, and our children's lives are within our reach. The proliferation of mobile computing and that little network of interconnected devices we call the internet offers the promise of making the world a bit smaller and more personal, making kids feel part of a powerful community that they proudly feel they have a hand in creating. But how do we help our students keep an even footing with their **digital footprints** on this new terrain, especially when it is terrain they feel they know so well that they needn't be careful? How do we help students use this dizzying array of new tools in focused, organized ways that empower them and engender the critical skills they will need for their lifetime? And how do we, as teachers, organize our own use of the internet to find greater focus in our professional lives and to help us inspire (*and be inspired*) by each other's best practices? How can we teach our students to take advantage of this wellspring of information and connectivity without it taking advantage of them?

Hello, World ... Meet Edmodo

Edmodo is one powerful answer. Like any good mission, Edmodo's is simply stated. Its goal is to "connect every learner with the people and resources they need to reach their potential" (edmodo.com/about, 2014). It is certainly not the only one, but Edmodo is by far the largest **educational social network** on earth and is flexible and robust enough to help unite many of these tools at our disposal for the betterment of our children, as well as for renewing and enriching our professional practices.

This book is intended to guide teachers, administrators, and parents to jumpstart (or expand) their successful integration of Edmodo into a learning environment. It is meant for both novices and veterans because, like Edmodo itself, this book has a low floor and a high ceiling, with easily accessible information yet lots of potential for even the experienced user to grow and learn new "hacks."

Our Experience

This look at the potentials of Edmodo is drawn from our own experience as well as the direct voices of hundreds of educators who share how this powerful educational social network can be used to supercharge the classroom experience and deepen learning and teaching.

More than two decades ago, our teaching careers began just at the advent of the World Wide Web. We were among the first internet-age technology trainers for the Los Angeles Unified School District, and so we guided classroom teachers in creating web presences in raw **HTML** and with early rudimentary **web editors**. We were inspired by the possibility these early web tools afforded teachers and students to express ideas and connect with one another, but it took a while for the tools to truly catch up with the aspiration.

In the past 20 years, we have worked in schools in five different countries helping to guide learning communities to maximize possibilities of technology for learning. As early adopters of Edmodo, we have been pleased to watch its expansion. Having led teachers and parents through the process of adopting Edmodo across learning communities, we have had the opportunity to use it in a variety of professional and personal capacities: as classroom teachers; as administrators, technology coaches, and directors; and as parents. In addition to using Edmodo with students in class-rooms, we have also had the benefit of enriching our own **professional learning networks** through interactions with other teachers and administrators in the online community. This is truly an exciting time for all of us in education. Now, with the widespread proliferation of classroom access to devices and the worldwide expansion of Edmodo, those initial aspirations are finally at all of our fingertips.

Using This Book

Edmodo can be used in a variety of ways, and there are clear benefits for all members of the learning community, all of which this book explores. In short, students gain the digital-age skill sets they need in a fun and safe environment. For teachers, Edmodo can help organize and enrich instruction and assessment; it can be a communication link among students, administration, and parents; and it can offer incredible opportunities for professional development. For administrators, Edmodo can be an important tool for facilitating greater communication and transparency in your learning community. Parents can use Edmodo to get a unique look into their children's classroom experience and be more informed about assignments and the general rhythm of classroom life.

The book also shows how Edmodo can be used as an instructional tool. We consider how it offers our classrooms a powerful way to integrate with a host of existing trends in education. From **project-based learning** and role-playing to **differentiated learning**, Edmodo can integrate seamlessly with many existing **class management systems** and instructional strategies. For those exploring the benefits of **gamification**, Edmodo offers a host of possibilities both with its available gamified apps and within the Edmodo interface itself, which can easily be leveraged as a role-playing/simulation tool and gamified space. Edmodo is also a powerful hub for the flipped or **blended classroom** as well as for a more traditional classroom enhanced with technology use.

Finally, we share how to create extensive professional learning networks using Edmodo to ask targeted questions, share your knowledge, find relevant resources, and create an extended network of colleagues with whom you can learn and expand together.

Features

Regardless of whether you are new to Edmodo or are an experienced user intent on expanding and maximizing your current use, you will benefit from the tips and techniques shared throughout the book, as well as the inspirational stories from other Edmodo users. The book offers the following features, each indicated with an icon:

Tales from the Trail

These inspiring quotes, stories, and ideas from real educators describe how Edmodo is currently benefiting their students and teaching practices.

Bright Ideas for All

These specific tips on smartly integrating Edmodo and making the most use of its varied features are helpful for newer users or those who want a refresher course.

Tips for the Power User

These tips are intended for experienced users who are ready to super-charge their Edmodo skills and take their practice to the next level.

How-to Directions

For both new and experienced users, these step-by-step directions help break down the steps necessary for easy navigation of Edmodo's many features.

Rounding out the book is a glossary for any unfamiliar or new-to-you terms. These terms appear in bold through the text and can be found in the glossary, which begins on page 113.

We begin now by introducing Edmodo and outlining the myriad of benefits teachers and students all around the globe are experiencing when they use this powerful tool. New users and those wanting a refresher will benefit from Chapter 2, which provides an orientation to the Edmodo interface. More seasoned users can skip ahead to the following chapters, which provide practical advice on integrating Edmodo and using it to its full potential.

Let the adventure begin!

Chapter 1

Understanding Edmodo and Its Benefits for Education

*E*dmodo is a unique **social network** designed especially for learning communities. When people try to describe it, they frequently call it "a Facebook for schools." This is true and it isn't. Edmodo certainly shares particular aspects with the world's largest social network, but at the same time, in very important ways, it is completely different.

Edmodo shares with Facebook a genius mission of humanizing and personalizing the vast resources of the internet, offering each of us our own accessible and organized unique portals for discovering information. At the same time, as educators we bristle a bit at comparisons to Facebook. We have all heard about young people who use poor judgment on Facebook and share embarrassing content of themselves that can never be completely taken back. Edmodo is dramatically different. It provides students a safe, protected educational experience, a place to safely practice the digital-age social networking and learning skills they will need in their increasingly connected personal, academic, and later professional lives.

A Snapshot of Edmodo's Current Use

In early 2011, Edmodo was the fastest-growing educational social network on earth, with just about 1 million users. A handful of months later the community of users had jumped to close to 7 million. In 2015, with 50 million plus users and counting—more than 85% of the largest school districts in the United States use Edmodo (Geron, 2012), and with teachers and students representing just about every country on earth—it shows no sign of slowing down.

With the host of benefits it offers teachers, students, administrators, and parents, it is easy to see why this educational social network has grown so quickly. Within the Edmodo platform, functionality is both simple and wide reaching for all the members of a learning community. Teachers create and lead **moderated** groups where students post questions, engage in discussion, and respond to instant polls or quizzes. Teachers can also immediately connect all around the world with other educators who are teaching the same units they are, share lessons, and find (and share) resources and lessons in the subjects that matter to them most. Students communicate with their teachers in new ways. They turn in their assignments in a paperless classroom, feel the pride of posting relevant content that they find to share with their class digitally, and showcase their work in a safe and protected environment. Administrators can communicate with their teachers and classroom in rich and intuitive ways. And parents, many for the first time, can get a bird's-eye view of some of the ways their children learn in the digital age.

Digital Life Training

I use Edmodo every day as my digital classroom. I give quizzes, post assignment reminders, share good news, and give my students access to notes and presentations in the folders section. A great site for getting your classroom ready with a 21st-century skill set in a safe environment.

Erin Montgomery, Teacher
Mansfield ISD, Texas

• • •

Benefits of Using Edmodo

Whether you are introducing Edmodo to one classroom or to an entire extended community of learners, it is helpful not only to know and understand the benefits of its use, but also to communicate those benefits to each user in your community, including students, administrators, parents, and fellow teachers. (Tips for communicating to your community are outlined in Chapter 3.) Here, we dive right into the important advantages of using the Edmodo platform.

Privacy: A Safe Space for Digital Learning

No data within the groups created inside of Edmodo are searchable from the general internet. Also, no personal information is required from any student. Teachers have complete control over what happens in their digital learning environment. They can moderate, edit, and delete any post by students. They can also control the amount of access that students have to their digital classrooms: whether students' posts need to be moderated, or whether they can post at all or are limited to reading posts by the teacher and/or other students.

Building Community

Edmodo has really helped to connect my students as classmates. They come to me in 6th grade from four different elementary schools and hardly know each other at all. Through the discussions on Edmodo, even the shyest student has a voice, which is saying quite a bit, since there are 120 students in my four classes! The environment in my online classroom is positive and friendly—and my students have been able to help each other remember to do assignments for my class as well as other classes, research for information needed on projects, review and evaluate each other's digital artifacts, and ask questions to which the answers are beneficial to the whole class.

Kari Salomon, Science Teacher
Hull Middle School

● ● ●

Empowerment: My Own Personalized Internet

The magnitude of the internet can be overwhelming, particularly for young learners. Edmodo invites a focused and personalized experience by attempting to make itself a one-stop point of contact for students' and teachers' interactions with the internet. In addition to directing their searches toward purposeful inquiry (as opposed to random or disoriented grasping into cyberspace), Edmodo has a growing armada of **embedded** applications (many free)—from tools such as Socrative (http://www. edmodo.com/home#/publisher/Socrative) which turns a classroom's existing devices into a set of smart, instant-response tools, to gamified apps such as CodeMonkey (http://www.edmodo.com/store/app/codemonkey-free), which uses playing games to introduce students to programming. These allow a wide range of curricular experiences without leaving the fold of the protected Edmodo environment.

Collaboration: Space to Share Ideas and Work Together

Edmodo offers numerous ways for students to develop collaborative skills. For example, teachers can empower students to have their own student-led collaborative reading groups. Each student has clearly defined alternating roles within the group, giving and responding to prompts that help them understand and interpret the assigned reading. In real time, students can see each other's live responses to the text. Importantly, this is combined with real face-to-face discussions about content. Students also see each other's posts to their class **stream**, and we all know how it changes the character of any communication and writing when we know there is an actual audience who will see the words. Students who might say anything on paper to "just get the job done" suddenly bring their best game knowing that their words immediately go live into the marketplace of ideas. For the teacher, monitoring the group affords an immediate bird's-eye view of student thought processes and helps to automate the gathering of assessment data.

Collaboration in Edmodo

I love that the students spend time socializing about learning. Very often a student will post a question to me about the assignment, and within 20 minutes five or ten of his or her classmates have answered the question and offered advice!

Christina Cagliostro, Teacher
Hyde Middle School

• • •

Edmodo can also be used to extend the student's **virtual classroom** to the rest of the world, further empowering and helping them to develop skills for professional and academic environments they will likely later encounter in life. All under a teacher's control, groups can be created with members (or guests) from anywhere. For example, students could have an extended discussion about *Lord of the Flies* with students in the Pacific Islands, who would bring to it the unique cultural knowledge that only they could share.

The Teacher Is in the Driver's Seat: Teacher Controls

Teachers manage the way their Edmodo environment is organized by their ability to control accounts and content.

Account Control

Teachers can choose the type of control individuals or class users are given in the following ways:

1. A regular Student Account, which gives students the ability to post and contribute to the class stream. Or,

2. A **Read-Only** Student Account, which allows students to read the teacher's and other contributing students' posts to the class stream, but doesn't allow them to post themselves. (Some teachers find this useful as students begin to use Edmodo and get used to it, or as a temporary measure if a student doesn't yet "get" the concept of proper **digital citizenship**.)

3. Teachers are given a private code when they set up a group that allows them to invite any teacher or student users to join their group.

4. Teachers can also control whether they want to moderate, that is, approve posts before they are visible on the class stream. (We don't necessarily recommend this added level of work on your part, but it is available.) Remember, you can be notified of all posts as they appear and can always delete a post if for some reason you feel it is not ready to appear on the stream.

Content Control

Teachers can, at any time:

1. Choose which students receive which content by giving all or select students access to **folders** and resources.

2. Instantly edit or delete student posts.

3. Control who sees what posts and when. Posts can be sent to specific groups or students and can, if you like, be scheduled to post at a specific time in the future.

4. Subscribe a particular group to an **RSS feed**.

● ● ●

Teachers can also tap into expert knowledge, inviting scientists and other professionals into temporary or long-term discussions with their classrooms in a safe, protected environment. For example, two teachers from learning institutions far apart in the world who want to collaborate on a specific project need only create a shared group in order to use Edmodo as an instant collaborative learning space.

Professional Development: Supporting and Expanding Teaching Practices

For those of us committed to making our learning communities even more successful, there is perhaps no more important factor than access to dynamic professional development networks. Edmodo offers uniquely targeted learning networks for teachers and administrators. Users can either tap into a host of existing groups and **communities**— focused on anything from project-based learning to the creation of a flipped classroom—or instantly create their own groups. Teachers can easily find and connect with others sharing similar interests, even those teaching the same units at the same time! They can share and discuss curricular knowledge and resources in unprecedented, focused, and targeted ways.

An Avenue for Shared Professional Growth

I use Edmodo as a means to encourage sharing and learning among the curriculum coordinators in the schools within our complex area. I reflect on and share links to web-based articles and resources of interest to these teacher leaders (and the teachers they support) as well as upload files on a variety of topics (in lieu of constantly attaching files to emails), including the handouts for our meetings. It is an avenue for my own professional growth in support to schools.

Wendy Heyd, Resource Teacher
Maui School District, Hawaii

Organization: Everything in One Place

Edmodo invites a host of organizational benefits for learning communities, from creating reusable quizzes and other content, to organizing multiple learning environments in one convenient interface. It also provides teachers with an efficient interface for reaching out to students when they are absent from school. The **Planner** function, besides its obvious benefits for the teacher in communicating homework assignments, allows for organization of in-class assignments, rubrics, and events. For students, creating their own digital planners allows them to develop personalized and organized relationships with their own learning. Adding their own events and tasks to their planners further personalizes their educational experience.

Differentiation: Custom-Fit Content for Your Students

With the ability to create unique groups and reusable content, Edmodo offers teachers convenient ways to differentiate content for the needs of individual students. Teachers can create small groups that are specific to student interest or ability, creating sequential folders of activities that are appropriate for specific student levels and ways of learning. Students in one group gain access to new content as their abilities progress, and students in another group receive resources that meet them where they are ready to learn.

Differentiation and the Common Core can be addressed and informed by the analytic features of Edmodo, which allow teachers to gain immediate data about their students' learning experiences. In particular, **Snapshot** is a tool within Edmodo that allows teachers to prepare students for specific Common Core State Standards (currently in English Language Arts [ELA] and Math). Described as a Common Core "micro-assessment" tool, it lets educators quickly generate formative assessments aligned with specific chosen Common Core Standard(s). This gives teachers a simple way to identify where students or classes need support for specific standards and where they have demonstrated mastery. By monitoring students' **Likes**, teachers can get an immediate *quicktake* of the most popular content, and depending on the prompt, see which students are excelling and which students self proclaim that they need additional help, and then use this data to direct students to differentiated content accordingly. The Snapshot and Likes features are described further in Chapter 5.

Giving Choices

Students check Edmodo every night for links and resources that I provide them as a way of differentiating their learning experiences and giving them choices.

Kari Salomon, Science Teacher
Hull Middle School

• • •

Authentic Communication: Writing for Real Audiences

Within a social network, students know that their ideas will become real to an authentic audience the instant they post their contributions to a live stream. They also understand that this dynamic stream morphs and changes as the teacher and other students interact with each other's ideas. This awareness encourages students' best performance and also tutors them in considering themselves as part of a dynamic extended community exploring questions and solving problems together.

No Pressure

Edmodo gives everyone a chance to respond with their ideas as well as alleviate any pressure from giving a "wrong" answer.

Nick McWhirter, Teacher
Twin Lakes School Corp, Monticello, Indiana

• • •

Engagement: Greater Classroom Efficiency and Rigor

Edmodo offers an easy and efficient way to communicate with students through such regular actions as giving feedback and creating alerts about assignments. As well, it furthers communication with the extended learning community of parents and administrators by offering them unique insights into what is happening in the classroom.

With all of these things in mind, Edmodo invites the unique potential for transparency, but it also encourages teachers to bring their best game to their own practice. Educators have the opportunity to offer the most rigorous learning experience by leveraging all these different capabilities—such as the ability to gain analytical insights into students as well as targeted access to curricular resources, matching them with the students that will benefit from them the most.

The ISTE Standards: Setting Goals and Realizing Potential

The ISTE National Educational Technology Standards are the roadmap for improving teaching, learning, and leading in a digital age. They help measure proficiency and set goals for what students, teachers, and administrators should know and be able to do with technology.

Edmodo dovetails nicely with the mission of the ISTE Standards and their focuses by providing:

- An authentic platform where students can share their creative work and comment on the work of their classmates, as well as a platform for engaging in simulations.

- A safe environment for authentic communication with one another.

- A powerful, focused tool for collaborative learning.

- A digital space to express and develop critical thinking and problem-solving skills—for example, as the student and teacher pose and respond to questions.

- Experiential knowledge of concepts and terminology, particularly social media.

- Guided practice in the rights and responsibilities of being a digital citizen within an ethical and responsible framework.

In many ways, Edmodo can serve as a hub to bring your experience with the ISTE Standards alive.

We have considered here how Edmodo can be a valuable tool for learning communities. Throughout the rest of the book, we consider its use as an instructional tool for all levels and capacities within a learning community. First, let's take a brief tour of Edmodo to familiarize you with the interface. Seasoned users may still find the following section helpful, as it includes reference to apps and practical examples, but they should feel free to skim or skip straight to Chapter 3.

Let's get going with our total integration of Edmodo!

Chapter 2

Navigating the Edmodo Interface

*E*dmodo offers a host of easy-to-use tools. In this section, we briefly survey the main tools you need for basic use, organized into the following categories:

- **Getting Started** (the basics of getting your accounts up and running)

- **Basic Functions** (what you need to know about simple use)

- **Classroom Essentials** (the tools that can help enrich the Edmodo classroom)

- **Organizational Tools** (the basic tools within Edmodo that help teachers and students keep their files at their fingertips)

Although you may find some new and valuable nuggets here, experienced folks might want to skip to the next chapter to discover ways to deepen your Edmodo practice. Given that Edmodo is consistently updating their interface, the appearance of some of the following features may change; however, their functionalities, and how to take advantage of them, remain the same. Let's get started!

Getting Started

Getting started with Edmodo is simple and free. Creating a teacher, school, or district account and using it with your students is free. (Premium paid accounts with additional features are available to schools and districts, see edmodo.com/districts for details.) Some apps within Edmodo are available for purchase; many others are free.

Setting Up an Account

At edmodo.com, specify whether you are a teacher or student, enter your email address, and come up with a unique password. You will then be asked to identify your school (there are also options for homeschoolers). If you are working with students eighth grade and under, you will be asked to provide some additional information, for security purposes, in order for you to be a fully verified Edmodo teacher.

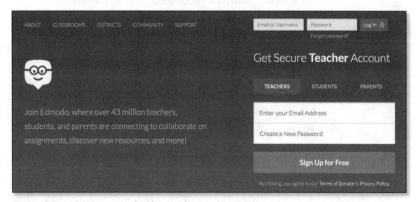

Figure 2.1 • Getting started with a teacher account

If your school already has a **subdomain** in Edmodo (e.g., CooltownElementary.edmodo.com), you will be going there instead. Check with your school site technology person if your school is already using Edmodo to be sure.

First Time User Quick Start Steps: The Essentials

1. Go to Edmodo.com.

2. Follow the steps to create your free teacher account.

3. Set up your teacher profile.

4. Create a group to start using with students (one for each of your sections/classes).

5. Familiarize yourself with the interface before introducing the tool to your students.

6. Create an opening prompt for students to instantly respond to in the group. A good one is to invite students to introduce themselves. Another could be posting a quotation, video, image, or article and asking students to respond to it. In fact, some teachers find this a great class opening strategy to continue with for every class session.

7. Make sure you have gone over **code of conduct** agreements for proper Edmodo use in your classroom. See the sample in Chapter 4.

8. Guide students in a class session to create their student accounts and profiles. They will now need the group code Edmodo generated when you formed the group. You can find this in your group settings.

● ● ●

Next, you will be instantly prompted to set up your class **groups**. You can do so now if you'd like, but you can always come back to add/change these later. Once you are finished, you can go to your homepage and get started finding communities you want to follow. You can check your progress under the account settings, where you will find a useful "done list" to make sure you have gone through all the necessary steps.

Setting up Profiles

Both teachers and students will be setting up profiles to identify themselves within Edmodo. You will set up your profile first, before introducing Edmodo to the students. Next, students create their accounts and set up a very basic profile. Set aside at least a good portion of your first class session with Edmodo to allow time for this. The profile itself consists of an associated image (or **avatar**) and a set of infor- mation students can associate with themselves, such as a career goal, a favorite quote from a preselected set, and their preferred learning modality. Edmodo keeps these aspects limited to make sure the information is appropriate for all learning commu- nities. The part of the profile in which students can best express themselves is their avatar image.

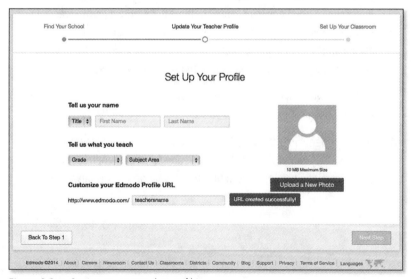

Figure 2.2 • Setting up your teacher profile

Students will have the opportunity to select from some images that are already available in Edmodo, but they will likely want to customize these further for a sense of ownership. We recommend that, as part of smart digital citizenship, you clearly state to the students that avatars are not photos of themselves. You may want to have a session in advance when students can design their own Edmodo avatar/icon. Depending on age level, this could be done using an editing program such as KidPix, Paint, or Photoshop or online graphic editors such as Pixlr (pixlr.com). (Profile images could also be hand-drawn images that have been scanned in.) Students also have the option of using Edmodo's profile avatar maker (see Figure 2.3) to build a customized avatar feature by feature (head, hair, eyes, etc.).

Figure 2.3 • The Edmodo avatar maker

These profile avatars will appear every single time the students post in Edmodo. We suggest that you set up some clear guidelines about what is appropriate in these images and whether you will require the students to only use public domain images. (Pics4learning.com offers a free image library for education.) You will want to make sure you set guidelines for acceptable images, because students may change their avatars periodically. Also, as part of giving teachers complete control, at any time the teacher can instantly remove a student's avatar. In a group, under Group Name, click Members. For the student in question, click the gear setting icon and choose "Remove Profile Image."

Getting Started Tips
When First Introducing Students to Edmodo

- Plan a regular login time for your students as they are getting started with Edmodo. No matter how savvy the students are with social media, some of them will undoubtedly forget their usernames and/or passwords. If you need to help a student access the username of their already created account, go to your group's homepage and click on Members. This gives you a list of all students' names, access rights, and usernames.

- If a student forgets his or her password, you won't be able to access it, but you can prompt the student to create a new one by clicking on Change Password next to that student's username in the Members view. The student can discreetly change it on your computer, click on Reset Password when done, and be off and running again. Incidentally, this is also where you would go if you ever needed to change the access rights of any of your contributing students.

- Let students know they can adjust the way they receive **notifications** of new posts inside their settings. Notifications can be turned off if students are overwhelmed by too many email messages all at once (if they provided a school email address when initially setting up their account).

- Be sure to stress right up front, on the first day you introduce Edmodo to students, that although there are many visual similarities to other social networks they are familiar with, no student is able to privately message another student. Be clear that, although this is not a problem at "our" school, the reason for this is to protect against possibilities of cyberbullying. Let them know that any resources relevant to the class they share will go directly onto the shared class stream. We have found that if this information is given clearly up front, the students are very understanding, but if this fact is introduced later in the process, students may be disappointed if there is a gap between their expectations from their own social media experience and their actual Edmodo experience.

● ● ●

Basic Functions

Posting

Students are able to post messages to the whole group or subgroup (see the next chapter for information about the functionality of subgroups) or their teacher. As a measure to protect against possibilities of cyberbullying, *no student is able to post or message another student in private.* In addition to regular postings, students can also attach media such as photos or videos to their posting (at present there is no file limit, although there is a limit per file of 100MB max). Students can also attach links from the **Backpack**. (Essentially a student library, the Backpack is further described in the Organizational Tools section of this chapter.)

Teachers have a lot more flexibility in their control of their own posting. In addition to posting to groups, teachers can also post directly to individual students as well as to the parents associated with any particular group who have signed up for parent accounts. In addition to posting messages and multimedia, teachers also have a variety of other ways they can post. By default, a post is automatically a note, but teachers can also choose it to be an alert, an assignment, a quiz, or a poll.

Figure 2.4 • The various types of teacher postings available in Edmodo

You can also choose when a message appears. By default, a message posts "now," but teachers can also choose to schedule the message to appear at a specific time or day in the future. Figure 2.5 shows you how the scheduling feature works. This is a useful tool if, for example, you want to send personalized messages to each of your students on their birthdays; you can schedule them all in advance at the beginning of the year. If you were creating a completely online class and knew in advance when certain assignments, polls, alerts, and so on, were supposed to appear, you could set these up in advance, essentially automating the class. For example, a pre-created quiz could automatically appear every Friday at noon. Those scheduled posts are easily accessible under your notifications if you need to alter them.

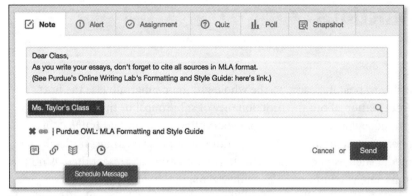

Figure 2.5 • Click on the clock image to schedule a post

Alerts

For quick important messages that teachers would like to highlight (e.g., a message about an upcoming test or class trip), they can post their messages as alerts. Teachers can choose to send them to all their teacher connections (see Chapter 3), all groups, or just an individual group. The process to create an alert is the same as posting any message, but once you select Alert, the posting will be highlighted, appearing in bold and showing up in student and parent notifications.

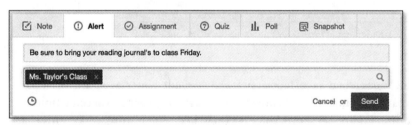

Figure 2.6 • Creating an alert

Figure 2.7 • The alert appears in bold on the stream

Classroom Essentials

Polls

Another type of message teachers can post is a poll. This is one of the simplest ways to instantly gauge class climate. Polls can be easily integrated into daily learning activities; for example, during a class lecture, students could be asked, "Are we moving: (A) too fast, (B) too slow, or (C) just about right?"

 Quick Steps to Create a Poll

1. Start a message just as you normally would for any post. Instead of the default option, Note, choose Poll.

2. Add a question. For example, how many hours a week do you use the internet?

3. Write in a couple of answer choices. Click on additional answer choices to add more options.

4. Choose which of your groups will receive the poll by starting to type the group name in the Send box.

5. Click Send.

6. The poll will appear to the group.

7. Results will appear immediately in the main stream as students take the poll.

8. Remind students that they may need to refresh their page to see the latest results.

• • •

This feature can also be used for interactive class polls and integrated into math assignments to show real-life graphing of data. It can also be a fun way to have instant class votes, such as voting for a student council representative, the next activity or book, themes, or wherever having a vote makes most sense for your learning community.

All of these polls are anonymous. If you are going to use polling to gather a vote, then in order to prevent students from being influenced by the crowd, have them all vote simultaneously and remind them that it may be necessary for them to refresh to see all the results. Your students will be excited by participating in live polls and seeing the instant results.

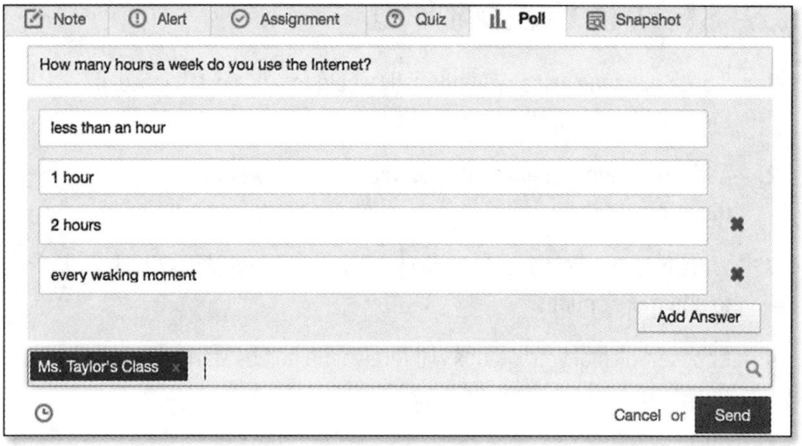

Figure 2.8 • Getting a poll ready

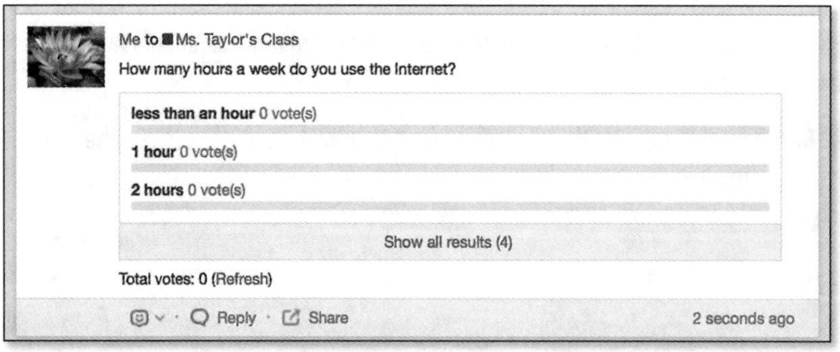

Figure 2.9 • A poll once it has posted

Assessment with English Language Learner (ELL) Students

I am a middle school teacher of ELL students. I use the quiz/polling features as exit slips in my classroom to assess student learning on the fly. I appreciate that scores are added directly to the grade book. I put the standard number in the quiz description box so I can readily see how students are performing by standard. Even though eight of my students speak little to no English, they have all been successful at following the intuitive prompts in the quizzes.

Ann Marie Palmer, Teacher
United States

Quizzes

A great feature within Edmodo is the ability to create embedded quizzes. These can be automatically graded and scores can be immediately posted into your grade book. You can also create a bank of questions to incorporate into other quizzes as well as a bank of quizzes to reuse. Quizzes can be multiple choice, true/false, short answer, or essay. Remember, if you choose short answer or essay, that will require you to go in later and grade them. Sticking to true/false and multiple choice means the grading is done automatically for you within Edmodo, based on your prewritten correct answers.

Figure 2.10 • The quiz interface

Differentiating Quizzes

If you want to further differentiate vocabulary, reading level, or content, you can assign different quizzes to particular students or subgroups within your group.

• • •

Filters

One benefit to using Edmodo in the classroom is that it provides a single organized repository and archive for a teacher's class, practice, and class interaction. And beyond simply acting as a repository of this material, Edmodo makes it easy to navigate by allowing students to drill down into class content to locate specific material. **Filters** allow you to search by author (teachers or students) or to just see your alerts, quizzes, polls, or latest RSS feeds. You can also filter by direct messages to the teacher.

Figure 2.11 • Different options for filters

Assignments

For those with the goal of moving toward a paperless classroom, Edmodo's **Assignment** feature makes that a real possibility. Completely within the Edmodo environment, you can create an assignment, link it to all the associated materials (e.g., rubrics), set a due date, and allow students to turn that assignment in virtually. If you like, you can also annotate student documents, provide students with immediate digital feedback, and instruct them to resubmit their final work. You can also use the "schedule a post" feature to have the assignment automatically post to students on a particular day and time. In this sense, you can set your circulation of assignments to be on autopilot so you can focus your energies on quality one-to-one engagement and feedback.

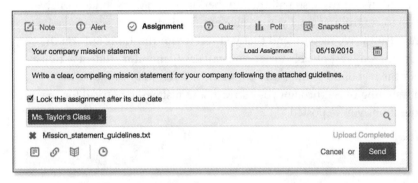

Figure 2.12 • Getting an assignment ready to post

 # A Class Repository

On the first day of each semester, my scholars are given their class code and we are off and running. I put everything on Edmodo! I have created shared folders that contain all of my PowerPoints, vocabulary, reading guides, and review materials among other things.

Lawrence J. Burns, Teacher
Northgate High School, Newnan, Georgia

• • •

Notifications

Notifications offer you real time updates on all your associated groups and communities. As with everything else in Edmodo, you, as the teacher, have complete control of the number and delivery of notifications. You can choose to receive notifications by email or text message, or just see them on the notification alert bar whenever you log in to Edmodo (this is the setting we choose in our accounts for almost all content).

As your use of Edmodo grows, so will the number of notifications. It pays to give some attention to controlling what you receive notifications about, and when, in your account settings. We recommend that you receive notifications only on the groups you are directly responsible for, so you can easily monitor student activity and posts. For the rest of the groups and communities you follow or join, we recommend watching those through your stream and just being notified for specific answers to questions you've posted.

Badges

Everybody likes to be recognized. A **badge** is a visual pat on the back, an award that you can use to recognize students for a particular level of achievement or specific accomplishment. Students see the badges they have earned in their profile.

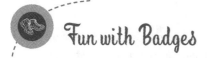

Fun with Badges

My students love receiving badges for participating, being a homework helper, a lookout, a wise owl, and even for beating the test with a 100. For a while we had a silly science joke page, and that helped get everyone on board. Students had fun with the Martian Calculator and earning badges for it.

Kari Salomon, Science Teacher
Hull Middle School

● ● ●

Badges can serve many purposes. They are powerful and convenient tools for assessment. They can easily be incorporated into your existing classroom management routines. And badges also offer an effective way for those interested in dipping their toes into gamification, which we discuss in Chapter 5.

Edmodo offers a host of premade badges, or you can create your own. You can even exchange badges. When you create a badge and its associated description, you can decide whether or not it can be made available to other teachers to use in their classes as well. Badges can be used to keep track of students' levels, of book groups, or in an extended class simulation. For example, badges used in a space mission simulation might be Captain, Commander, and Communication Specialist. Or, if you have progressive modules that students complete, they can "level up" with the badges. Edmodo also makes it easy to award badges to multiple students at once. In the Gradebook/**Progress** screen, shown in Figure 2.13, you can see at a glance all students' awarded badges.

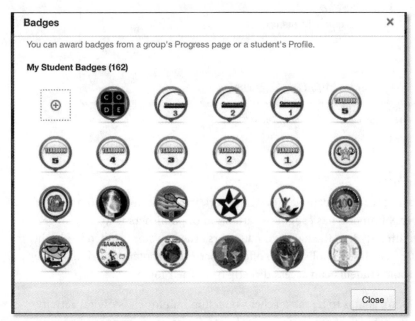

Figure 2.13 • Student badges

Likes

Within any group in Edmodo, you can get a sense of most popular shared content, and, by monitoring students' 'Likes' of particular posts, gauge class mood, etc. Along with other data, this can help you better understand the ever-changing realities and needs of your learning communities.

Figure 2.14 • The number of Likes are shown below each post

Edmodo Apps

As the most successful educational social network in human history (in terms of sheer numbers), Edmodo has caught the attention of publishers who want to get their content directly into the hands of educators. The app store embedded in the Edmodo interface allows publishers to offer subscription content (much of it free) that teachers and students can access directly from their login.

Part of Edmodo's goal is to be the teacher's one-stop hub for class digital activity. An important part of that are these internal apps. Some of the apps specifically align with standards, such as Common Core, AERO, or Next Generation Science Standards. Accessed through the students' Edmodo **App Launcher**, these games and learning modules can be reached without ever leaving Edmodo.

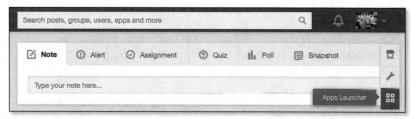

Figure 2.15 • Link to the App Launcher

In our discussion of differentiated learning in Chapter 5, we will talk about strategies to keep track of student work. Many of these apps have their own internal systems that keep track of students' progress. Many are also automatically embedded in your grade book. Both allow wonderful benefits for your class management system. Many of the apps also automatically provide students with badges as they complete particular tasks or modules.

Because there are many Edmodo apps and the list is growing rapidly, we highlight only a few here that have cross-age and cross-disciplinary appeal.

10 Edmodo Apps to Customize Your Learning Space

1. **Socrative** (http://www.edmodo.com/home#/publisher/Socrative)

   Socrative is a self-proclaimed "smart **student response system**." Teachers can create multiple-choice or short-answer quizzes, exit tickets, or single-question activities, all of which can be shared with other teachers. *(Free)*

2. **instaGrok** (http://www.edmodo.com/home#/store/app/instagrok-lite)

   The instaGrok app is designed to help students develop research skills in an adjustable environment based on interest and necessary levels of ease or difficulty. It is an interactive search engine for learners, the results of which

Continued

are displayed visually as a web of main concepts and their relationships. Built-in journals allow teachers to track student progress. *(Free and ad-free paid versions)*

3. **Blendspace** (http://www.edmodo.com/home#/store/app/blendspace)

    Formally known as EdCanvas, Blendspace is an app for teachers to easily create content particularly for **blended learning** environments. *(Free)*

4. **CodeMonkey** (http://www.edmodo.com/store/app/codemonkey-free)

    CodeMonkey is a game for teaching K–8 students to program simple code. *(Free and paid versions)*

5. **Subtext** (http://www.edmodo.com/home#/store/app/subtext)

    Subtext allows a group to engage in a collaborative discussion around any digital text. Great for content area articles or reading groups developing skills in close reading, critical analysis, and writing skills. *(Free)*

6. **Class Charts** (http://www.edmodo.com/home#/store/app/class-charts)

    Class Charts is a class management app that allows teachers across classes/ schedules to create multiple seating charts or groups, provide students feedback, and track behavior progress. Class Charts reports can be shared with the student and parent accounts, making for instant and increased communication. *(Free)*

7. **eduClipper** (http://www.edmodo.com/home#/store/app/educlipper)

    eduClipper is a **social bookmarking** app that allows users to easily "clip," collect, share, and control the digital content (websites, images, videos, articles, etc.) that students, parents, and colleagues see in their stream. It also allows professional learning communities to easily share resources and collaborate in real time. *(Free)*

8. **Digital Passport**
   (https://www.edmodo.com/home#/store/app/digital-passport)
   Digital Passport is an app that presents the powerful digital citizenship content by Common Sense Media through videos, interactive games, and activities. *(Paid)*

9. **Pixton** (http://www.edmodo.com/home#/store/app/pixton-comic-maker-trial)
   Pixton allows students to create interactive comics to demonstrate their understanding of a concept or idea. *(Free and paid versions)*

10. **Curriculet** (http://www.edmodo.com/home#/store/app/curriculet)
    Curriculet offers hundreds of free and ready to use, editable "curriculets" (curriculum-enriched texts that include both instruction and assessment). The app also offers Common Core aligned materials. *(Free)*

● ● ●

You can access and browse available apps (organized by subject) in the Edmodo app store. Click on the Store button, shown in Figure 2.16. You can browse available apps by Subject, Free, Most Popular, and Recently Added.

Figure 2.16 • Link to the app store

Getting Apps

From the store, identify an app you would like. Next, click the Install App button and choose the group(s) you would like the app to be associated with. An example is shown in Figure 2.17. (If there is a cost associated with the app, you will need to have applied credit to your account.) Whenever any student associated with the group clicks on their app launcher, they will see any games, apps, or modules you have added to that particular group. App providers generally also have an associated community that you can follow, post a question to, or use to network with other teachers using that particular tool.

Figure 2.17 • Installing an app in your group(s)

Organizational Tools

Groups

Groups are one of the most important concepts within Edmodo and make it especially flexible and powerful to use. As a teacher, think of a group as a specific digital classroom where you basically have complete control. You decide who gets in, and whether they can actively participate or only listen. You can even lock the doors if and when you would like to close enrollment. The uses of these digital groups are as many and varied as for the formation of any group in a physical classroom.

Before we talk about some ideas for how to use groups, let's quickly consider the mechanics of how a group works. As a teacher, you simply create a new group on your interface homepage. Click on Create and name the group. If you would like, you can identify a grade range and a subject area. You can also identify expected group size, if you have one, and have the group automatically close enrollment when you have reached your specified goal.

Once the group is created, circulate the Join URL or Group Code (Figure 2.18) and ask students to join the group. As students join, they will populate your list of members by default. Anyone added will automatically have full student participation rights. At your discretion, you can limit a student's access (or that of a whole group) to "read only" status. If you do not want students to be able to automatically join the group with that code, you can also circulate the "request to join URL" link. Then you will get a notice whenever anyone would like to join, and you can accept or deny. Best practices dictate locking the group once you have populated it with intended members (this happens automatically after 2 weeks). You can always unlock it if you want to, but locking the group ensures that you will not get unintended members if the unique code accidentally becomes compromised.

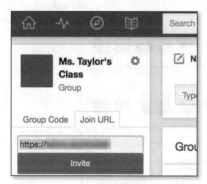

Figure 2.18 • Circulate the Join URL to invite users to your group

Now that you have populated your group, you can share particular folders of resources, create assignments, and subscribe your group to an RSS feed (see Chapter 3 for more on RSS feeds and ideas for using them in the classroom). You can also automatically see all of the content your students have created and have control of editing or deleting if you see content that is not consistent with your Edmodo group guidelines. It is reassuring to know that here you have as much control of the content as you like.

In addition to groups that students join themselves, you also have the ability to easily place students into smaller specific groups within a larger group. This can be useful for student-moderated discussion groups about a book, cooperative learning groups, or specific content-related groups such as a science fair team. The possibilities are endless. Once you have students in one of your larger groups, it is easy to move them around into these smaller groups.

Communities

Communities offer a great way to connect and share resources with other teachers or administrators. Within Edmodo there are vast communities for specific curricular areas (such as math, science, or professional development) in which you can network, seek and find advice, share resources, and get informed answers to your questions. Although anyone can create a group, and there are perhaps thousands of them out there, there are a comparatively small number of communities. And whereas a group may have only a handful of teachers, communities can have tens (if not hundreds) of thousands of members. Communities are basically sorted into two major areas: specific subjects such as computer technology, career and tech education, and support, and publisher communities, such as ISTE and Khan Academy. Both become a great bank of searchable conversations and resources in addition to living resources to interact with regarding concerns and successes.

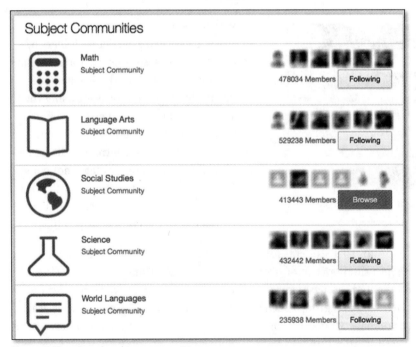

Figure 2.19 • Sample subject communities

Edmodo for Everything

My class uses Edmodo for almost every aspect of learning. They view videos for their nightly homework, take quizzes, ask questions of me and their classmates, retrieve documents, turn in assignments, provide peer feedback on essays, etc. Everything the student needs is in one place. It has also reduced my grading time significantly. I no longer have to hand-grade quizzes or worry about misplacing papers.

Amanda Kerschen, Teacher
Uplift North Hills Preparatory, Irving, Texas

● ● ●

Library

Edmodo bills the **Library** feature as "your own virtual library that you can access anywhere and share with anyone." It offers "unlimited space" to organize documents and multimedia objects for teachers to share or keep for future reference. Any object can easily be shared into the particular folders associated with any of your groups. Think of this as your grand repository of material. As you browse communities, posts, and groups, a handy feature of Edmodo is that it allows you to automatically add these items to your library for later reference.

Figure 2.20 • The Library helps you organize your documents in one place

How to Add to Your Library

You can add to your library with any post, by clicking the gear setting icon to the right of the post and choosing Add to Library, or clicking the Add to Library button next to any content you find interesting. Alternatively, you can upload any of your content directly to your library.

Backpack

The Backpack is virtually identical to the Library, but it is made for students. They can use it as their "virtual flash drive." Many schools have found this to be a useful way to eliminate the "promiscuous" use of flash drives on the school network and the potential vulnerabilities that allows. The Backpack feature is also an easy way to share material between home and school. In addition, both the Library and the Backpack can be linked to your Google Drive, which makes for even more efficient integration for classrooms and schools already using Google Apps.

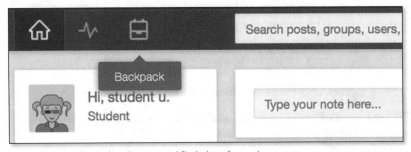

Figure 2.21 • The Backpack is a virtual flash drive for students

Planner

The Planner feature allows a teacher or student to see all their upcoming events, assignments, and projects for all groups in one place. They can also add their own tasks and events. Click on the Planner button 30 within the apps toolbar on the right side of the page. Then, in a glance you can:

1. See all your assignments and events for all groups.

2. Switch from a weekly to monthly view of your assignments, events, and tasks.

3. Select the assignments or events for just one group by clicking on the ∨.

4. Add a new event or task by clicking on the +.

5. Export or print the Planner by clicking on the gear settings icon.

6. Keep a to-do or personal check-list or wish-list by adding a new task to the Someday section.

These are the ways in which Edmodo seeks to be a one-stop digital learning environment. Whether you are seeking to create a paperless classroom, a gamified one, or a flipped environment, the built-in flexibility here can help promote a dynamic and organized digital space for you and your students. Now that you know how to drive Edmodo, in the next chapter, we consider some of the possible instructional paths as you map your journey.

Figure 2.22 • The Planner allows you to view upcoming events and assignments from all of the groups you teach as well as those in your professional learning communities. You can also keep a list of your tasks.

Saving Time and Paper!

Edmodo has allowed me to cut my paper usage by 90%. This is one of the aspects of Edmodo that I appreciate the most. Students today are technologically savvy and embrace Edmodo. I love the fact that when I post assignments, they are saved in Edmodo. All I have to do the following semester is click on the assignment and it (along with any attachments) is automatically set up. All I have to do is change the due date and I am good to go!

Lawrence J. Burns, Teacher
Northgate High School, Newnan, Georgia

Chapter 3

Integrating Edmodo

𝒩 ow that we know what Edmodo is and what its benefits are for students, teachers, administrators, and parents, we turn to specific ways it can aid instruction. Edmodo is an incredibly versatile tool that can easily meet the needs of dynamic elementary, middle, and high school learning communities. Moreover, it can serve as a valuable means of communicating learning processes with parents. We take time here to consider each of these in turn, as well as to discuss the power of Edmodo for teachers connecting and networking with their professional learning communities.

As we discuss the various grade/age levels of use with Edmodo, you will find that many of these will overlap. You know what is best for your class. You may find that regardless of your students' age, they appear to be ready for some of the activities, tips, and scenarios suggested for another level. For example, one that is recommended for middle school may be perfect for your fourth or fifth grade classroom or for a high school class. So let's get started and go to school with Edmodo!

A Critical Tool

I have been using Edmodo for 4 years. I began using it as a communication tool between myself and my students and their parents. I now use it primarily to assign quizzes, tests, and student responses to debatable topics. Since our school lost funding for a keyboarding program, I also find myself using it this year for real-world typing practice. I typically pose a question and require the students to create constructed responses or blogs. It also allows students opportunities to respond to other's views or opinions. It works great for homework help and allows the students to take initiative when they need help with homework or an assignment they may had left at school. It is a critical tool that helps my students succeed in and out of the classroom.

Shauna Geary, Early Childhood and Gifted/Talented Teacher
Chesapeake Public Schools

• • •

Using Edmodo with Elementary Students

Safe Social Networking

In many ways, the strongest benefit Edmodo offers is for older elementary students using it as a safe **digital learning** community. However, even for early elementary school students who are not yet ready to take the leap to engage in this educational social network, Edmodo can still serve as a valuable tool.

Communicating with Parents

Even the earliest grades, prekindergarten and kindergarten classes, can take advantage of Edmodo's capability for connecting with parents. Although students would normally create their own accounts, for the youngest children it is smartest for the teachers to create the accounts for them and simply use the accounts as a communication tool with parents. In practice, what this looks like is leveraging all of your existing parent communication and using Edmodo as a hub for it.

Although the parent account functionality at the time of this writing is limited, it still offers a powerful way to give parents a glimpse into the daily life of a classroom and an organized forum to communicate class life to them. We think it would be ideal if there were an option for parents to be able to communicate directly with the teacher and to let them provide ongoing feedback to class events, but these are things Edmodo does not do. It does, however, give most parents a wealth of information they otherwise would not have about their child's academic life. Edmodo can be a one-stop shop for teachers to share photos and video of classroom activities with brief descriptions, post class newsletters and calendars of classroom events, give individualized feedback to students, recognize achievements, and (if applicable for your grade level and/or school) send out home and extended learning projects.

Tip: For Those Serving Communities with Limited Internet Access

Although internet access is becoming more and more widespread throughout the world and in all communities, we suggest that schools open up their media centers and libraries before and after school to families with limited or no internet access at home. This way, Edmodo can easily reach everyone in your learning community.

• • •

At the early elementary level, Edmodo can be used as a well-organized method of communicating information about early childhood development or other information a teacher might share during the course of the year. A teacher can post links and files for parents to read or download that pertain to specific lessons taught in class or information and articles for how to further support their children. One early childhood teacher shares that she uses Edmodo primarily as a way to get information out to the parents about topics that are of interest as the year goes on. It is an easy place of focus to organize a year's worth of information that parents can easily refer back to later.

Classroom Management

Another way to leverage Edmodo is to use it as an organized hub for classroom management. One teacher reports, "I think it is a more efficient use of my time than filling out certificates for kids. I can give regular feedback to parents about how their child's day was through the use of the badges, which I can create myself."

For students who might be placed on a behavior contract or other method of classroom management, the badges offer a space to do that and have regular communication about it. The e-badges never get lost, and the parent, student, and teacher can all access them when they need to.

A Tool to Grow With

As children grow in their elementary years, the functionality of Edmodo grows with them. It goes from being primarily a means to push information out to parents to being a tool students can use themselves in the classroom and at home. By this age, students have developed the digital toolset (basic keyboarding and some basic understanding of digital communication) as well as basic reading and writing that help them navigate Edmodo more independently. Students are ready to take advantage of Edmodo as a vibrant digital community. In some ways, this is the best time to introduce Edmodo, because they are excited about the shift and it lays the groundwork for important skills that will serve them for the remainder of their digital life.

Sharing Ideas

Edmodo can serve elementary-age students and teachers in many ways as a tool for learning and engagement. By allowing students to respond to prompts posted by teachers, provide reactions and answer polls, Edmodo can give the teacher quick insights into students' affective states, and foster discussions that give all students a voice. At this and every age, Edmodo offers a wonderful way to appropriate students' love of passing notes and bring it into the entire classroom experience as well as leverage it as a means of assessment. Teachers can maximize this through joint story creation and even digital role-playing, where students pretend to take on certain roles they might have just researched or give responses based on the knowledge of a particular animal: a conversation between frogs, anyone?

A Communication Hub

I use Edmodo for communication between myself and my students, and for my students to communicate and collaborate with each other. I also post reminders about concerts or assignments they have, as well as giving them assignments they can hand in on Edmodo.

Cristina Betancourt, Middle School Teacher
Riverside District 96

Using Edmodo with Middle School Students

Middle school is a time when students' bodies are going through dramatic changes—and so are their digital lives. In many ways, the capabilities of Edmodo as a learning tool and environment blossom completely in middle school. At this age, perhaps more than any, students need and can truly take advantage of the kind of safe, protected practice in social networking that Edmodo affords.

Modeling Good Digital Citizenship

Digital citizenship, by which we mean the norms of appropriate, responsible behavior with regard to technology use, becomes much more of an urgent concern in middle school. By necessity, Edmodo becomes an ideal place for extended units about digital citizenship. (Some of the best available can be found through the Common Sense Media resources in the Common Sense Media Publisher Community.)

Staying in Sync from Anywhere

Teachers in my school post homework, remind their students of tests and project due dates. They use it effectively for students who have been absent. The student can go right to the homework assignments (and possibly classwork) and have it all done by the time they come back to school, thus not missing a beat!

Jo Stone, Teacher
Johnson Middle School, Bradenton, Florida

• • •

Edmodo also becomes an ideal place to take advantage of much of the independence that students of middle school age are ready for in the regular classroom. With Edmodo, they can practice this in the digital form as well as through student-moderated reading, math, science, music, art, and other content-related groups. These offer a great way to take advantage of Edmodo's small-group function. Small cooperative groups with clearly defined functions—for example, reporter, facilitator, coach, or resource manager—can generate and respond to their own prompts about specific assigned texts and do so in a way that is completely archived. In this way, they serve as part of the continuing growing resource bank of the classroom, created by the students.

Edmodo is a great way to communicate homework or last-minute changes in assignments and to send rubrics or other information, even after your students have left your classroom for the day. Teachers can dynamically share any news in their Edmodo class stream, but at the same time the news can also be organized for later reference in class folders in the student's library.

Set Up Office Hours

On the note of communicating with students in Edmodo, especially as we reach the middle school level, it is important that teachers announce up front that they will only be available and communicating with Edmodo during school hours (regardless of how often they actually check in). This will prevent a great deal of possible misunderstanding in the future, as well as offer teachers more well-earned shuteye.

● ● ●

Using Edmodo with High School Students

Many of the uses we have already discussed also apply to the high school setting—particularly independent student-moderated groups, analyzing text, driving content, and taking part in flipped classrooms, as well as extended simulations and immersive language experiments (such as requiring all posted discussion in whatever the particular language of instruction is, such as Spanish). In addition to all of these things, Edmodo can offer unique benefits for the high school learning community. Most especially, at this level, there is an opportunity to push out higher level content to older students.

Letting Students Take the Lead

Edmodo has allowed me to be more of a facilitator of learning in class since my students have been accustomed to discussing with and learning from each other, making the learning more in-depth and student-centered.

Corazon Libao, Teacher
Garland High School

● ● ●

How to Change Your Language Settings

The entire Edmodo interface can be changed into more than 10 languages, including English, Spanish, French, Greek, Chinese, Turkish, German, Swedish, Portuguese, and Dutch:

1. Go to the bottom of any page in Edmodo.

2. Click on the word "Languages" in the bottom right corner of the page.

3. Choose a language.

• • •

RSS Feeds

RSS typically stands for Really Simple Syndication. In general, it allows a user to subscribe to an internet site, podcast, or other content so that you can receive new content as it appears. For example, whenever breaking news appears on the Wired Magazine site, if you have subscribed to its RSS feed, you will see it. This process usually requires an RSS reader.

Any Edmodo page can serve as your RSS reader. Therefore, any Edmodo group can be subscribed to any available feed. By doing so, the process becomes automatic. Any new content to that feed will automatically go to that group. So, for example, a science class may automatically receive up-to-date news items of the latest science findings of the world. To maximize this, students can have regular assignments where they then need to summarize or respond to the content of relevant articles in a journal section of that science class. For example, students would need to choose one article each week from the page for a response. Ambitious teachers could also generate short quizzes in Edmodo based on particular articles and have them automatically graded and posted into the grade book.

Depending on the feed, there might be occasional content that you may not feel is wholly appropriate for your class. Although it may be valuable to use RSS feeds, and they can be a rich way of extending the class, you need to keep your feed moderated, occasionally weeding out ones you feel are not appropriate or relevant. Also note that the frequency of the articles will depend on the source, which could range anywhere from one a week to several a day.

Although RSS feeds could be used at the middle school level, they are a particularly great way of pushing specific curricular content to high school students.

How to Subscribe Your Edmodo Groups to an RSS Feed

It is easy to jump right in and subscribe any of your groups to an RSS feed. Here's how:

Find the Feed

1. Get the RSS feed for a site whose content you want to follow. For example, for the Wired Magazine feed, go to Wired.com and click on the RSS icon.

2. Once you have clicked on the icon, all the available feeds to subscribe to will appear. Click on the one you want to get the link for the feed (it will usually have the word "feed" at the beginning or the end).

Subscribe Your Edmodo Page to the Feed

3. Go into your Edmodo homepage for any group.

4. Click on the group settings (the gear icon).

5. Click on Subscribe to RSS Feed.

6. Paste in the feed link you gathered in Step 2.

7. Click Subscribe.

Now whenever new content appears, it will be pushed out to that group's page stream.

• • •

A Good Feedback System

I use Edmodo as a tool in my chemistry classes mainly to submit lab reports. I also like to give short quizzes and polls to provide myself with feedback on certain activities and topics we cover. I also like that I can provide interesting links to students that can help them within the chemistry courses I teach, and I love the alert system to remind them to study for tests! Edmodo also provides a medium for my online "office hours" where students can Q/A and get immediate responses to questions.

Kerry Townsend, Teacher
Scottsboro High School, Alabama

• • •

Alternative Learning Groups and Homeschooling

You don't need to be in a traditional school setting to take advantage of all that Edmodo has to offer. Edmodo has vast offerings for homeschoolers and those working with students in other types of learning environments to connect, post announcements, communicate their calendars, track student progress, and share resources. When you create your teacher account, just click on the link for Homeschool or Higher Education, and you are off and running creating groups, quizzes, polls, and interacting in real time with your homeschooling or alternative learning community. Edmodo's flexibility can have a great deal to offer regardless of the type of learning environment.

A Group Just for Us

Having a group formed for just Catholic schools was awesome during the season of Christmas (Advent) because there were many ideas discussed that I was able to incorporate during my reading group time.

The world of education and learning got even better when Edmodo became available!

Karen Krestchmann, L.D. Reading Teacher, K–4
St. Louis Catholic School, Batesville, Indiana

• • •

Using Edmodo as a Communication Tool with Parents

Both parents and teachers can appreciate what Edmodo can do for school communication. Through the use of the Edmodo Parent app for mobile devices or their home computer, parents are certainly in a unique position to benefit from the use of Edmodo in any school or classroom.

Some great ways to use Edmodo as a parent communication tool include posting the following:

- Newsletters

- Archives of previous newsletters

- Classroom activity documents so parents can be more intimate with the details of your lessons

- Photos and video clips of the classroom activities

- A calendar of upcoming events

- Communication about homework

- Individual praise for their students

- Congratulations for their students on new badges, which could also include behavioral charts or other organization systems to support student achievement

- Alerts to parents—for example, reminders about special days or events

- Links to sites, videos, or articles you want to share with parents.

A Worldwide Professional Learning Network

The ability to interact with other teachers through the various communities on Edmodo is a great benefit. It is like having a professional learning network at your fingertips 24/7! I recently made a post with a question and heard from a teacher in Argentina! Having a worldwide professional learning network just cannot be beat!

Lawrence J. Burns
Newnan, GA Northgate HS Coweta County School System

• • •

Using Edmodo to Network with Other Teachers

Just as Facebook's success is largely based on successfully personalizing people's experience of the internet, Edmodo's meteoric rise is largely due to its ability to do the same for teachers. Where once we faced a sea of seemingly limitless but difficult-to-pinpoint resources, Edmodo provides teachers powerful yet simple ways both to zero in on teacher-tested resources and also to join (and form) dynamic networks with others in and out of their fields or subjects.

In general, there are five basic ways for teachers and administrators to connect on Edmodo: joining existing teacher-created groups; creating your own teacher groups; joining subject and publisher communities; direct communications through teacher connections; and using the **Spotlight** tool to pinpoint connections specific to what you are teaching this moment.

Group Code Netiquette

It is generally considered poor form to ever directly share a group code in any public forum, including the communities. Group codes are shared offline or through prepared teacher group lists. Get a sense from that individual community about their protocol for sharing and promoting relevant group codes and be respectful of that. In general, freely circulate the "request to join" URL instead. That URL can then be posted and circulated in any social media, Twitter, Facebook, and so on.

● ● ●

There are hosts of specific teacher-created groups, where teachers interested in or with experience in a particular area connect to share resources and experiences and ask questions. In addition to these existing teacher groups, as an Edmodo teacher, you can effortlessly create your own new group, no matter how specific. For example, teachers interested in educational uses of circus arts in science can just start their own group if one does not already exist. After creating the group, you share the group code (or preferably an "invite to join group" link) in the relevant community. You have instantly created a group of similarly interested teachers from throughout the world.

In addition to these, communities are a great place to begin to develop your professional learning networks with Edmodo. These are divided within general subject areas as well as in publisher communities, such as Khan Academy, where publishers often share free resources with educators. You may find that these communities are sufficient for your networking needs. Within them, library resources can help you narrow your search. They are also a great place to find out about more specific teacher groups that exist. Lists of teacher codes are regularly shared with the larger subject communities (such as math, science, language arts, and computer technology). These communities are also great places to announce your own new groups in the relevant forum. For example, your group of circus art science connections may be relevant to both the science community and the arts community. Let them both know!

In some ways the most powerful way to extend your professional learning network through Edmodo is by use of the Spotlight tool.

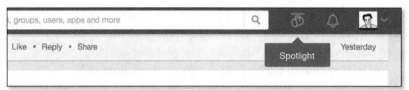

Figure 3.1 • Click on the Spotlight button to uncover new resources and make connections

This tool allows you to zero in on what you are teaching at any given moment and instantly both (1) discover the most popular and widely shared resources in Edmodo at any given moment connected to that, and (2) find individual educators who are teaching the same thing at that moment, offering you a powerful opportunity to make new teacher connections. Teacher connections are direct requests to connect in with another Edmodo educator. Rather than randomly requesting people because you like their name or avatar, you can use Spotlight to identify a precise pool of other educators, presumably teaching the same content you are, and to initiate potentially mutually beneficial connections.

This host of tools is among the best immediately available in our digital world for teachers to create and extend their own professional learning networks. In the next chapter, we put all these tools to work for you as you introduce them to your community.

Chapter 4

Kicking Off Edmodo in Your School or Classroom

a successful launch into the school community can be crucial in integrating Edmodo into active use in your school learning community. Making sure that all the stakeholders are on board and understand the basics of Edmodo's host of features and benefits is not difficult—but it is crucial to your success.

In this chapter, we provide some basic suggestions for explaining Edmodo and creating enthusiasm for it in your classroom and/or larger school community. Many of you reading this will be concerned with getting started with Edmodo in your own classroom. The folks at Edmodo make launching it in your classroom incredibly easy.

Prepared rollout material is available on their site (support.edmodo.com) and comes complete with introductory letters to parents, training materials, summary overviews, and relevant PowerPoint presentations. That is your first stop. Rather than duplicating that here, we will give you other suggestions, assuming that you will also take advantage of the valuable resources Edmodo offers in your startup phase.

Getting Started

If you have the luxury of doing so, start early—*very early*. Well before you plan to introduce Edmodo, plant some seeds. Let parents and others know that this great tool will be coming down the pipeline soon. Once you are actually launching Edmodo, your key objective is to make sure that all the stakeholders have a realistic understanding of what it is as well as its benefits and limitations.

Introducing Edmodo to Your Students

In introducing Edmodo to students, generate enthusiasm while making expectations for its use extremely clear. It is essential that everyone begin on the same page about what kind of content is appropriate and allowed in your Edmodo classroom. We strongly recommend that before the students ever post, you provide a code of conduct and review it with them. Edmodo provides basic guidelines for digital citizenship, but you know your students best; you will likely want to customize it to the unique needs of your class or school. Form 4.1 shows a code of conduct that we have used with our students. Depending on your grade level and learning needs in your class, you will want to modify it further.

We strongly recommend that you begin with fairly tight reins. Although you can always loosen the reins later, it is extremely difficult to tighten them after the horses have left the stable. For example, some teachers start all students in read-only mode until they have signed their agreement to honor an Edmodo Code of Conduct. See Chapter 1 for more information about read-only mode.

EDMODO CODE OF CONDUCT

1. I will use a respectful tone of voice when posting. My conduct in this digital community will continue to be consistent with the existing (your school's name) Code of Conduct.

2. I will use appropriate grammar instead of texting language. This includes correct spelling and grammar. (Occasional errors are acceptable—nobody's perfect—but language should be appropriate for a classroom discussion.)

3. All links and content posted should be relevant to class discussions/assignments. I will not use my posts to promote personal websites or chat rooms.

4. I will not reveal any personal information on Edmodo. This includes telephone numbers, addresses, emails, etc. (Even though this is a private social network, it is still on the internet, and we should follow general safe internet use guidelines.)

5. I will not post photos or videos showing my classmates or myself without permission.

Date _____   Student Signature _____

Form 4.1 • Sample code of conduct

Older kids, middle school and up, will definitely want to use Edmodo in the same way they use other social media. Although it is essential to leverage their enthusiasm and knowledge of social media tools, it is at least equally important that they clearly understand how this is different from other social media tools, especially for those who are regular Facebook users.

First, we strongly recommend that texting language *not* be allowed in any Edmodo communication. Some educators may disagree, and for older students, perhaps in high school, we see valuable discussions that could happen regarding ways to use texting language. In general, though, Edmodo can be framed as an extension of classroom discussions. Regardless of what grumblings students may have about not being able to use texting language here, they understand that there is different language for friends on the playground than is used in a class discussion.

Once your students have spent a good deal of time in Edmodo and have demonstrated appropriate behavior, you may consider having a special group that can be an off-topic "hallway room" or "student lounge" where students can feel free to talk about off-topic things such as movies; they would at the same time be made aware that it is a teacher-moderated group. We personally chose not to do this, and most parents support the idea of keeping Edmodo use clearly academic.

Regardless of whether you decide to keep your students' Edmodo use strictly academic or not, it is essential to give the students a sense of ownership of their Edmodo environment and encourage authentic, meaningful use in and out of the classroom. A key part of this is encouraging students to customize their profiles. For digital literacy reasons, we begin by insisting that students limit themselves to avatar images they create themselves or that are in the public domain (e.g., from pics4learning.com).

Top Reasons to Establish a Code of Conduct

1. A preestablished code of conduct is proactive, as opposed to being reactive.

2. Having a code of conduct in place minimizes the time a teacher will need to spend on policing posts.

3. A code of conduct offers the students comfortable boundaries, which helps create an environment conducive to fun and active learning, where everyone feels safe and heard.

4. A code of conduct sets students on the right path for lifelong, positive digital citizenship.

● ● ●

Other ways you can encourage a sense of ownership include having your students log in frequently to get familiar with the terrain of *Edmodo-ville*. You may even allow students an opportunity to be involved in badge design. Teachers around the globe are reporting that the Edmodo platform helps give all students a voice, boosts confidence, and helps keep students more organized. Students will quickly take ownership with a few simple steps that get them off and running in the right direction in their new digital environment.

The following steps assume that your school has in place an acceptable use policy (AUP) or that you have already let parents know you will be creating age-appropriate social media and have their permission to do so. (If you do not have an acceptable use policy, you can talk with your administrator about using one. A nice template for an AUP is available at Lightspeed Systems: (archive.lightspeedsystems.com/resources/Acceptable-Use-Policies.aspx).

Steps for Introducing Edmodo to Your Students

1. Sign up yourself.

2. Have an age-appropriate discussion about what Edmodo is and how it will be used in your classroom.

3. For older students, have them sign up for their accounts all together in class.

4. For younger students (ages 8 and under), we recommend creating the accounts for them (again, make sure parents are clearly informed/have provided consent for the process).

5. Have your students post an introduction consistent with the rules or classroom agreements. Delete any posts that are inconsistent with these agreements (texting language, etc.) and highlight models where students are doing it "right." (You could quietly pull aside kids whose posts did not make the cut and explain to them why.)

Continued

6. Plan a tour of the features in Edmodo.

7. Send a letter home about how this has been introduced and the enthusiasm around exploring it.

8. Start finding simple ways to bring Edmodo into the kind of class activities you are already doing. If you are lucky enough to be part of a one-to-one program and your students have ready access, you could do simple things like having them check in *(post what you plan to do this session)* at the beginning and check out *(what did you do?)* at the end of all class sessions to help establish comfort with Edmodo.

9. Keep your administrator in the loop about you are doing. Be sure to also let them know about benefits for them as an administrator, such as greater classroom transparency, organization, and safe digital citizenship practice for students. Your use may well encourage schoolwide adoption.

10. The key strategy for success with Edmodo is simple: regular Edmodo use in your classroom. *Go slow and steady to go fast* is our motto.

● ● ●

Introducing Edmodo to Parents

Although Edmodo provides introductory letters that can be shared with parents, you may wish to create your own in order to establish connection with parents or add a personalized touch. Form 4.2 is an example letter similar to what we have used. You may want to wait to invite direct parent participation until you (and/or other teachers) have had time to practice, use, and get comfortable with Edmodo.

Dear Parents,

This year, we will be using Edmodo in our classrooms. Edmodo is a free and secure educational social network for teachers, students, and schools. It provides a safe and easy way for us to connect, share content, and access home learning projects, other assignments, and school notices.

Edmodo also offers parent accounts, and we would like to invite you to join us online. With parent accounts, you can view your child's homework assignments and due dates and receive updates on class and school events.

To join your child's classroom in Edmodo, follow these steps:

1. Go to *[Type in your school's unique Edmodo address before sharing the letter.]*

2. Select "Parent Signup" (The link is located below the student and teacher signup buttons.)

3. Key in your unique code(s) in the Parent Code field (either received from the teacher or found in your child's account on the left side of the home page just beneath Groups and Communities under the banner "Parent Code"), then create your unique username and password.

4. Select Sign Up, then your account is ready.

After you sign up for the first time, you will no longer need that parent code. From then on, you'll just log in using the unique username and password that you create.

Feel free to contact me if you have any questions. We also have an Edmodo mentor parent team made up of one parent from each class. These parents (listed below) have received some additional training and have kindly agreed to be another class resource for parents signing up and beginning to use Edmodo:

[List parent helpers here]

We hope Edmodo will help serve as a valuable communication tool for our learning community.

Best,

Albert J. Einstein, Teacher

Form 4.2 • Sample introductory parent letter

Edmodo Mentor Groups

Depending on the size of your community, you may want to consider forming an Edmodo mentor group of parents. This is a group of classroom parents for whom you provide additional training and resources so that they can then be an additional resource for other parents coming to Edmodo for the first time. The benefits to you as the teacher or administrator would be that these mentors would act as a buffer for questions that might otherwise come to you. It is the "Ask Three Before Me" model for parents. These parent mentors can also act as evangelists within the class for the possibilities of Edmodo. Above all, as you begin, be responsive to the inevitable questions that will come from parents. Be supportive, and help them keep clear on what the benefits are for their children.

● ● ●

Training Teachers in the Use of Edmodo

This last section of this chapter is assuming you are an administrator, a technology director or integrator, or a teacher leader introducing this useful tool to your colleagues.

Edmodo does a great deal to support teacher training. Part of the rollout kit that we mentioned earlier includes clear training materials to get teachers started (see support.edmodo.com). With some extra tips and good organization, you can successfully bring teachers on board. It won't take long for their enthusiasm to grow as they experience the benefits in their own classrooms.

Steps to Get Your Teachers Trained in Edmodo

Here are some basic steps to get you started. These can be done in general sessions, one extended session, or regularly scheduled meetings. In addition, of course, you will want to check in with teachers to evaluate their use of Edmodo and provide ongoing support even once they are off and running.

1. Introduce everyone to the benefits (for students and teachers).

2. Schedule a session where you can guide your faculty in account signup and joining a training group that you create.

3. Give an overview tour of the major features and benefits to using them.

4. Have everyone practice looking at Edmodo through students' eyes, seeing how it would be used in class (give your training group polls, quizzes, and start specific, targeted discussion groups).

5. Share resources within an Edmodo folder.

6. Introduce everyone to the support community where they can follow up and get more responses. This is especially important if the school does not have staff that can allocate time to provide regular support.

7. Share resources within the training group (consider adding an RSS feed of relevant professional development resources).

8. Post some of Edmodo's standard help materials and guides in a shared accessible place, both physically (such as posted to a board in a staff room) and digitally.

9. Send out regular ideas and tips to everyone and share successes in yours and others' classes.

10. Encourage administration to incorporate Edmodo into the school's ongoing professional development strategies.

• • •

Slow and Steady Teacher Tip

I suggest the teacher disable the post comments ability until the students get used to the routine of using Edmodo as a tool and not a social chat space without boundaries.

Naomi Rodriguez Timmons, Middle School Teacher & Technology Integrator
Lago Vista ISD

• • •

Now that you have introduced Edmodo to students and staff, let the fun begin!

Tip: Host an Edmodo Day!

Although introducing Edmodo to a classroom or community is usually done over the course of weeks or months, you can generate a great deal of excitement and awareness by having a designated Edmodo Day. This would be a good day to have after you've already incorporated Edmodo into your classroom. Here are some things you could do on Edmodo Day:

- Post a giant student-created poster (with a giant 'E') that says *"We're using Edmodo in our learning. … Ask us how."* Add student and teacher quotes (handwritten or printed) about how Edmodo benefits them.

- Appoint Edmodo Ambassadors who wear "Ask Me" buttons and prepare that group with talking points.

- Circulate student-created fliers describing Edmodo's benefits and ways students use it.

- Within Edmodo, host a contest (poll) or a game with a mystery to solve (with clues posted to a small group). How about some prizes?

• • •

Chapter 5

Taking Edmodo Farther in the Classroom

We have mentioned some of the ways Edmodo lends itself to instructional strategies. In this chapter we explore in greater detail how this powerful tool can inform your teaching practice. Many of the strategies presented in this book can be adapted to other different and complementary learning systems that you might be using as an educator. We focus here on Edmodo because we feel it is an especially robust learning system and has, as the great Seymour Papert has said of the best tech tools, a very low floor (easy entrance) and extremely high ceiling (potentials for use).

Edmodo and Project-based Learning

Edmodo can enhance almost all of the aspects that can make project-based learning (PBL) effective. The interface lends itself well to inviting students to engage and communicate in collaborative and authentic projects. For example, responding to a teacher post, a seventh grade middle school class can collaboratively generate a list of digital citizenship guidelines for younger students. With the list, students create a final product that they then teach to younger students and physically post in their classrooms. The outcome is that the creators (the older students) have internalized the digital citizenship guidelines much more than if they had merely read an article about it.

Although groups are at the heart of Edmodo, the small-group feature is perfect for project-based learning. As we have mentioned, the small-group feature allows teachers to easily cluster their existing students into identified groups. To give students a sense of ownership, let the groups define who they are, choose their own names, invite them to answer a meaningful question, and they can be off and running in their own collaborative digital workspace. An example of different small groups within Edmodo is shown in Figure 5.1.

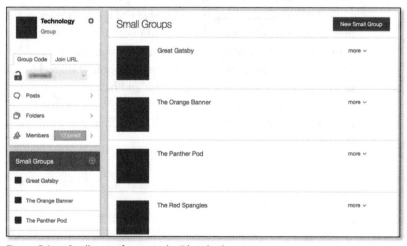

Figure 5.1 • Small-group feature in the Edmodo classroom

Edmodo can be a valuable tool for some of the biggest challenges project-based learning presents, such as assessment and organization. Unlike discrete assignments and tasks such as worksheets, which lend themselves easily to tracking and assessment, a true authentic project has a multitude of simultaneous tasks that are often unique to each group member.

 *Archiving*

Although the main stream of the class offers a great place to archive and communicate the daily happenings of your class through daily posting of your agenda and assignments (which you can easily invite parents to follow), the archiving feature allows you to essentially disable and archive groups that are not immediately active. You can still reference them anytime. They will appear under your group list under Archived Groups. Like an old friend, or bad luggage, nothing is ever lost in Edmodo. Once classes are complete for the term or year, you can easily archive them and have at the ready an organized reference to all the materials used and a snapshot of the learning that took place.

• • •

The small-group feature is a clear and organized way to keep track of all the elements each small group creates in one central hub for later (and ongoing) review by the teacher. Perhaps most importantly, students can immediately access and review these elements as they collaborate in real time. This gives students greater control of their own learning. Of course, small groups are excellent for creating student-moderated reading groups with assigned member responsibilities (e.g., moderator, question-prompter, recorder).

Even more, these reading groups can easily be morphed into project-based learning groups. Extended discussions about a work can be directed toward the creation of a final end product that students identify and design themselves and that clearly demonstrates their deep engagement with that work. For example, after spirited discussion and back and forth with students, a *Lord of the Flies* reading group has a record of their own created, shared questions, and their group becomes the hub for the creation of their own short film, housing their collaborative work on storyboarding, scripting, and the finished film.

Getting Organized: Check-ins and Check-outs

Many of the features in Edmodo make it especially well suited for a project-based, small-group scenario. At the beginning of every class session, students can be required to check in. This can be done as a quick gauge of their affective status, but for classes engaged in projects, it gives the students an opportunity to identify discrete tasks they need to complete in a particular session as well as practice communicating that. (See an example check-in prompt in Figure 5.2.) Of course, clearly articulating necessary action steps for each work session is a valuable skill for students to develop and make habitual. The more a person can develop organizational tools that they *live* and that become part of their daily educational life, the more likely these are to "stick" in their later academic, personal, and professional lives.

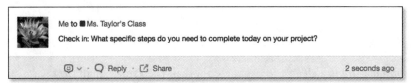

Figure 5.2 • Checking in as a way to jump start project-based learning

In addition to the value of these check-ins to organize a learning session, requiring a check-out at the end of the session gives students a valuable opportunity to reflect on what was accomplished in that session. They also offer students and teachers a quick opportunity to sketch out a few "breadcrumbs" to immediately follow up on in their next session.

In many ways, groups make the classroom teacher's job in managing projects not only easier, but also more effective. You and your students are likely to find the habits of check-ins and check-outs that Edmodo facilitates to be a valuable part of your project-based learning environment. We should quickly note that if you don't necessarily want to get as involved in the check-ins and check-outs as we have described here, these can also be done with quick polls that could be standardized, such as general statements students can choose from that help communicate their progress as a team. Examples might be daily choices ranging from: "My group was extremely productive this session," to "We stumbled and fell today … please help!" to anything in between. See Chapter 2 if you need a quick refresher on how to add a poll.

A simple way to add check-ins to your class is to make a post each day that says, "Today I feel… ." and invite students to quickly respond by adding a comment or word. Similarly, an effective check-out could ask the students to react to 'I had a productive session' with a Like if that is accurate for them. (Hovering over the 'Like' link on any post will show you the names of students who have 'Liked' a particular post). These are a few ways that check-ins and check-outs can help create a more synergistic and effective learning environment, allowing everyone to be truly present and aware of the feeling state of the other learners in their communities. This creates a learning environment that is not only more personally connected, but also more efficient—one in which students and teachers are better able to work together and understand each other.

Figure 5.3 • Using "Likes" to further understand your learning community

Tips for Creating Check-ins and Check-outs

1. Before the students arrive, have an opening post for them to respond to ready on their class stream. From your homepage, in the note box type the prompt–for example, *Today's Check-in: List the tasks you need to complete in this session.* Or, *Today's Check-in: What is your 1–2 sentence response to this article/video/quotation/image?* Under the prompt, type the name of the class group(s) to whom you wish to send the prompt.

2. Add content. You can add a link or file or something from your library to this post. Click on the File, Link, or Library button if you want to add content to the check-in or check-out.

3. Click on the clock icon if you would like either the check-in or check-out to appear at a particular time. For example, your check-out can be scheduled to appear 15 minutes before your class ends.

4. After students have written their posts, be sure to spend a moment to highlight at least a couple of student responses (if not all) to the whole class so that students know that you consider these posts important and are taking time to validate them.

5. Ten to 15 minutes before your class ends, have your students respond to a check-out. Your check-out could range from a quick self-evaluation of how each student did during the session (for example, on a scale of 1–5), to a report on their group or individual progress, what tasks were completed and what their next steps are.

● ● ●

Edmodo and Differentiated Instruction

As a flexible and real-time learning space, Edmodo lends itself especially well to differentiated instruction. Folders can be used to set up modules of sequential activities. A simple way to do this is to number the items in a particular folder so that the tasks are to be clearly done in sequence. Another good idea is to shift the "work" here of identifying useful resources to the (older) students and have them set up folders of learning modules for themselves.

When the Teacher's Away

I especially appreciate the ability to take my lessons and communication beyond the classroom with Edmodo. Primarily, I see Edmodo as a great tool for classroom flipping and differentiation. Edmodo allows students to work at their own pace, but still within deadlines, even if they are homebound, in ISS/DAEP, or have a substitute teacher.

Joelle Dulaney, Teacher
Richards HS/ISD, Richards, Texas

• • •

Through a reflection check-in (see previous section in this chapter), students keep track of their own progress. This could also be done as a daily assignment that requires students to post their plan and accomplishments for the day. Here, again, the check-ins and check-outs can be a great way to organize student work in a differentiated classroom. This could be done in combination with the modules the students are choosing from, or from their own identified tasks based on directions that you have previously approved. In connection with this, to help guide students' movement in the digital space, you could post a daily menu of activities, perhaps identifying with an asterisk some that must be completed, or other electives they can choose from. You, of course, know your class best, and depending on your class's age level, you may find that it works best to do this on a weekly basis, or at some other interval that best meets your class's needs.

Badges can also provide a useful means of letting students keep track of their progress and "leveling up" (as we will see in our gamification discussion), as they move through their own unique learning path. Figure 5.4 shows a progress screen displaying student badges earned. If it makes most sense for your content, this progress may not be sequential numbers but perhaps a series of badges that invite the kids to think spatially. For example, head, torso, arms, legs, or perhaps the rooms in a building, or other ways that invite students to see paths better reflective of your content. Badges can also recognize performance in their group roles, such as a "Great Questions!" badge.

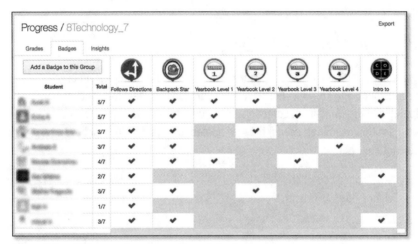

Figure 5.4 • Badges used to progress through levels of content

Connecting with Web 2.0 Tools

Whatever the existing Web 2.0 tools you are currently using, such as Blendspace, WeVideo, VoiceThread, Padlet, or Glogster, the daily active stream of Edmodo provides a place to showcase the immediate creations of your learning community. Many of these 2.0 tools (like Socrative, GoAnimate, and Khan Academy) are conveniently embedded in Edmodo, which makes it an especially convenient hub for your class's educational life. For example, a Padlet (padlet.com) that students have created as a visual collage or brainstorm of possible final projects for their reading of *Charlotte's Web* can be circulated as a link on your daily stream. Also, any tool that offers an embed code as a share option can easily be integrated into your daily stream, folders, and modules (just paste the embed code as a link).

Efficient Edmodo

I use Edmodo for my students to turn in any digital creations such as stop-motion videos, Google presentations, PowerPoints, Prezis, or other bodies of work that are similar. It allows me to access them from one location easily, and it prevents the hassle of the student trying to email a file that is too large or having to bring in a flash drive. It also makes presentations of student work a snap. I can open Edmodo and give the student the Mimio stylus. They can open the project, present their work, and then pass the stylus to the next student. With just a click, the next student is ready to go.

Kerrie Swepston, Teacher
Lorena High School, Lorena, Texas

• • •

Edmodo and the 1:1 Program

Many schools have embraced the promise of the 1:1 classroom, where every child has access to their own "personal digital assistant." Edmodo can help students better organize use of their 1:1 device, and many of the features we have discussed so far are also useful in the 1:1 classroom. As with differentiated and project-based learning, daily check-ins (where students identify what tasks they will do in a particular session, or their affective states), and daily check-outs (where students reflect on what they have accomplished as well as clearly defined next steps) are a wonderful feature for the 1:1 program, because students all have instant access and everyone can chime in all at once.

The Sound of (Edmodo) Silence

I have a class set of iPods and iPads. When introducing the tool of Edmodo and how to use it, I have a "Silent Day" lesson. The only way I communicate to the students, and them to me, is through Edmodo. Students log into their group and I submit questions about the topic as a note. They can only reply as a note and must ask three questions during the class. They are required to answer at least two other person's question. Kids love it. The silence is deafening while the posting is loud.

Robert Maw, Teacher/Technology Director
Carson Middle School, Carson City, Nevada

• • •

A Great Time-Saver

The app launcher can be a useful hub of activity in the 1:1 program, directing activity so students are not randomly searching the web. If students have been given a clear list of tasks to complete, they can do so safely from within Edmodo. Taking advantage of the fact that each child in the room has a device, an alternative to clickers (student-response systems) would be the app Socrative, which allows instant interactive ways to get feedback from your students (among other features). Of course, an abbreviated way to do this is by using quick polls. These polls take on power when students have their own devices at the ready and you can check in on them at any time to get a quick reading.

Edmodo can also be a way to maintain a cohesive sense of community, even if the class members are dispersed around the campus (or the world) doing different research tasks or activities. Edmodo can be a valuable addition to the 1:1 classroom in this way. Whether for 1:1 planning stages, early implementation, or seasoned use, many of the other topics discussed in this book can be very helpful in the 1:1 classroom.

Finally, a key part of implementing, maintaining, and pushing a 1:1 program further is the existence of active and invigorated professional learning networks. Edmodo lends itself to this beautifully, and its teacher communities and groups can be a key part of the blossoming of your 1:1 program. In its early stages, a clear discussion of the use of Edmodo can help administrators and teachers envision how they will use these digital assistants in their room. In turn, this can contribute to the organized and focused use and success of the 1:1 program.

Edmodo with Tablets, Phones, and Other Mobile Devices

Edmodo offers simplified versions of the interface in mobile device format. For the teacher, it offers a convenient way to quickly check in to class climate and activity through notifications wherever you are. Through the settings of your device you can, at your preference, set how you will receive notifications of activity. It also offers a quick way on the fly, over coffee or wherever you are, to quickly post agendas for upcoming class activity or to add web links and other resources to your class stream. Run your class from the beach in the Bahamas on your "sick day." We won't tell.

Mobile devices are also a way to quickly add photos or video taken with your device to your class stream. Gone are the days when you had to hassle with cords, plug in a camera, download the images, and then upload again. With the Edmodo app for iPhone, iPad, and Android, sharing media becomes an instant process and a valuable addition to your stream to build class community, communicate with parent groups, and add to your own documentation of class activity.

Edmodo and Digital Citizenship: Minding Our Digital Footprints

One of the greatest things Edmodo can offer educators is a safe, protected environment in which a learning community can master best practices for digital citizenship. Eric Schmidt, executive chairman of Google, argues quite convincingly that in the future of today's students, in many realms, students' online identities will be more important that their physical ones (Schmidt, 2013). For this reason, it is essential for students to have a clear sense of how to best manage their digital selves.

Many students don't fully appreciate the consequences and importance of their own posts. In recent polls among university admissions offices in the United States, a third admitted to checking the online profiles and activity of prospective students. Even more concerning, a third of those came across material that made them feel, "Hey, we don't want this kid at our school!" (Kaplan, 2012). If any generation needed more skills in digital citizenship, it is this one.

Fortunately, Edmodo's protected environment offers much of what is great about popular social networks like Facebook: the chance to immediately connect with those who are most important to you, to share information, and to make the vast possibilities of the internet a bit more digestible and familiar. Of course, it does this while protecting students from some of the potential pitfalls that other social networks can offer. Within Edmodo, unlike other networks, no student is ever able to directly and privately message another student; further, all of their digital content, although always made public to the whole class, is not searchable to others publicly on the web.

A key part of nurturing students who are reflective about their digital conduct within the online environment is beginning with a clear set of digital-use guidelines and community agreements. The folks at Edmodo make this easy, as they have already developed a basic set of guidelines. See Chapter 4 for tips about introducing Edmodo with a code of conduct and your students' digital citizenship in mind. As necessary, remind students of these agreements and safe practices and bring their attention to any that you find need any further attention. Don't forget that as the teacher, you can change the access rights of any student. If a particular student has trouble remembering to be respectful to other students, he or she can be placed (only temporarily, one hopes) in read-only status.

To heighten students' digital literacy skills, encourage them to make regular use of the filters to find relevant posts, and encourage them to comment on each other's continual compliance with your shared digital space agreements.

Truly, Edmodo is a continual exercise, offering daily options for ongoing practice in digital citizenship. Edmodo's structure allows all of this practice to take place under the helpful eye of an interested teacher, one who can help guide students as budding digital citizens and help create good digital habits that will, ideally, stick.

The Nine Elements of Digital Citizenship and How They Can Be Addressed in Edmodo

The nine elements of digital citizenship, created by author Mike Ribble, break down the concept of digital citizenship into themes for discussion and practice (for more information see digitalcitizenship.org). Edmodo is the perfect forum in which to explore the nine elements with your students. The following questions, each tied to one of the nine elements, can help frame your students' involvement and help make them reflective about their own citizenship in a digital world. A simple way to use them is to post these suggested questions as discussion starters sprinkled throughout the term in your main stream.

1. **Digital Access–Electronic participation**
   Does everyone in our community have equal access to digital resources? Does everyone in the world? How might it change a person's life if they never had access to the internet? How might it change your life? Your schoolwork?

2. **Digital Commerce–Electronic buying and selling**
   What are smart precautions to take when buying and selling goods online? (Commonsensemedia.org offers a good site for students to consider smart decision making in various e-commerce scenarios as well as other digital citizenship topics.)

Continued

3. **Digital Communication–Exchange of information**
   What are some of the tools we use to communicate digitally as 21st-century citizens? Think about one. What are the appropriate decisions we need to make with this tool?

4. **Digital Literacy–Teaching and learning about technology**
   How do you use technology to learn? How do you learn about technology? What kind of information literacy skills do we need? What do we need to learn? How do we learn new things? What are the most important skill sets we need as *21st-century* citizens?

5. **Digital Etiquette–Shared standards of conduct**
   What are best practices for polite and responsible conduct in our shared digital spaces like Edmodo?

6. **Digital Law**
   What are laws and ethic/moral rules we should be aware of and follow? Are these laws different in different places/countries? And for different ages?

7. **Digital Rights and Responsibilities**
   What are the rights we have as digital citizens? What are the responsibilities that we have as digital citizens? How are these two connected?

8. **Digital Health and Wellness–Using technology in ways consistent with physical and psychological health and well-being**
   How can the internet be good for our health? How can it hurt us? What physical-health and psychological issues should we be aware of and protect ourselves against when we use technology, including ergonomic concerns?

9. **Digital Security (Self-protection)–Precautions to take for safety**
   What are smart ways to protect our information? For example, virus protection and backing up data, and protecting your online identity. (Ribble, 2014)

● ● ●

Edmodo and Gamification

One of the most important emerging trends in commerce and education is gamification. In its simplest terms, this refers to adding game elements and game thinking in non-game environments to a learning situation to encourage problem solving and deepen engagement in learning. Game designer and gaming advocate Jane McGonigal convincingly argues that much of our assumptions about games and gaming "as a big waster of time" doesn't give us the full picture on why games are so popular. McGonigal asserts that the main reason kids like games is because they give us the things that all humans want: hard work; "blissful" productivity with clear, immediate visual feedback that encourages community and meaningful collaboration; and "epic meaning" (some cohesive narrative that lets kids participate in something larger than themselves) (McGonigal, 2010).

Game On!

I use Edmodo to flip and gamify my seventh grade Talented and Gifted ELA classes. I post all of my Trainings (homework), Quests (assignments), and Bosses (tests) in Edmodo. I also award my students with badges, and we create a leaderboard based on their XP (experience points). Students also collaborate with each and other and myself on various quests. We have also had the opportunity to collaborate with students from other states as well as in various book clubs. Edmodo has definitely redefined how I engage and instruct my students, and it has been fantastic to say the least.

Timonious Downing, Teacher/Technology Director
Walker Mill Middle School, Prince George's County Public Schools

● ● ●

So how can we leverage our students' existing literacy with games to deepen their engagement in the classroom? Companies are integrating gamification in ways that are so commonplace that we don't even notice them. For a simple example, when you purchase an item on Amazon, you follow a status bar along the top that creates a clear visual narrative, from putting an item in your basket through to completing your purchase: you have just been gamified. You have been placed in a clear narrative that guides your behavior. It makes you want to get to that last step! You are more likely to follow through with the tasks if you know exactly where you are in the process.

Here are a few basic strategies to help you use Edmodo to gamify your learning spaces:

Leveling Up with Badges

Games often reveal new content or environments as students show achievement. This is called "leveling up." Just as badges offer you a great visual way to recognize student achievement, they can also be used to indicate a student's leveling up. So, your badges could say Level 1, Level 2, and so on as you go through the content. If you want to get creative, you could have new badge images appear with each new level. Students can get excited about discovering the new levels and their associated images. As we said, there are simple elements of gamification everywhere. This is just another way to meet our students where their experience lies and make their learning environment more meaningful and connected to their everyday life.

Simulation Toolkit

One way to think of Edmodo as a resource for gamification is as an inventory of tools that you can customize and use in your **simulation**, or gamified learning environment. So for example, a student is awarded a "key" badge and then the teacher simultaneously grants the code or moves them into a small group that has access to a folder that has specific content (in its main stream and/or folders) that they have now "unlocked." So now that you have opened a new group, that group may also have new folders, connected to new content, and new tools that help them move through the simulation.

Missions

A key idea inside gamification is framing ideas and tasks in a meaningful narrative. A simple way that this is done is framing an activity or assignment as a **mission**, a larger goal encompassing smaller related tasks, by incorporating the following elements into your Edmodo classroom.

A Visual Map

It may be helpful to design, or have your students design, a visual map of your mission, such as a house with four rooms (or a map of an imaginary place or a location from a relevant story, such as the world of Narnia). Then you create a group that becomes each room. In each room, students discover content you have placed in the folders. That content could be a variety of types of media: videos, images, articles, and other Web 2.0 content specific to that concept. Now your students need to explore each part of the territory and complete the related mission or quests. For encouragement, let them earn badges on the way. They will be having the kind of fun that learning was made for.

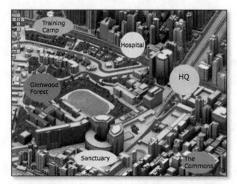

Figure 5.5 • Visual map where students uncover missions. Each map "location" can correspond to a content folder.

Easter Eggs: The Value of Searching for Worthless Treasures

Easter egg is an old computer coding term. It basically means non-purposeful, fun content that encourages exploration. In early video games, clicking on some object in the room could possibly reveal some hidden message or image that has no real relevance in the game but is "cool" to discover. Knowing that this content is there and that only the savvy will find it makes it even more desirable for some students on their quest. The way that we use this is by having surprise content appear when students go through a folder of links. Students learn that they may discover some kind of fun, goofy content that engages them in their current cultural literacy, such as a zombie clown or a funny clip of old Wile E. Coyote. Students will be inclined to thoroughly explore all content knowing they might occasionally stumble on one of these purposeless gems! It is amazing how engaged they will become because they know there are buried treasures along the way.

• • •

Designing a Game

At its simplest, a game is a set of rules that set up artificial obstacles to completing something. Think of the game hide-and-seek. The purpose is to "seek" your friends and uncover them in their hidden spaces. The unnecessary obstacles are that they will hide, you have to close your eyes, count to ten, maybe spin around to disorient yourself, and that they can also run if you spot them.

Framing It All as a Story

As your class goes on its missions and quests, place it all in within a story. Framing your learning game with some basic narrative (perhaps a class trip to the moon) gives the game and content greater purpose in the eyes and experience of the student. For maximum engagement, involve your students in generating ideas for the narrative and some of the obstacles for your game.

Extended Simulations

Deepening your narrative provides great opportunities for students to take on roles in a simulated environment. Student and teacher profile images can be temporarily changed to resemble characters from the narrative. Folders or badges can be named for the geographical features of the setting. Posts can be in the voice of the various characters. The possibilities are endless.

All of these ideas basically present to the students what games offer: organized productive work and the opportunity for specific feedback and awareness of their level of achievement. And it is done in such a way that calls on spatial thinking, and a sense of fun to deepen engagement.

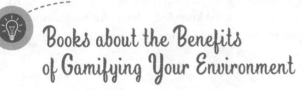

Books about the Benefits of Gamifying Your Environment

Reality Is Broken by Jane McGonigal

The Multiplayer Classroom: Designing Coursework as a Game by Lee Sheldon

Why Video Games are Good for Your Soul: Pleasure and Learning by James Paul Gee

For those interested in deepening their understanding of gamification, the best-known course is offered free through Stanford University (coursera.org/course/gamification).

Edmodo and the Flipped Classroom

For those brave (and smart) souls who have flipped or are flipping their classrooms, Edmodo is a fantastic tool that seems almost perfectly designed for everything that is great about the flipped classroom. Edmodo supports and/or extends every reason why one would flip their classroom. Jonathan Bergmann and Aaron Sams are educators and authors who have helped revolutionize many classrooms with the simple beauty of their model. Basically, in the flipped classroom, low-level content knowledge is "flipped" out of the classroom, and students learn it independently through videos, screencasts, and other digital material that they see on their own, principally at home, freeing up face-to-face time for more genuine teacher-student and student-student interaction. Class time becomes a time for clarifying questions, and an opportunity for engaged collaborative problem solving and project activity, informed by the students' shared front-loaded knowledge base. Although aspects of this have been done for many years, as a defined model, the flipped classroom is new.

Flipping Edmodo

In my "flipped" United States History classroom, I use Edmodo as a platform to post my video lectures, as well as to create quizzes for my students to complete to make sure that they are grasping the material covered in the video. I have also used Edmodo for students to participate in blogging assignments, where they are required not only to post their opinion about a particular topic, but to respond to other student comments as well. Students are able to easily communicate with me through Edmodo to catch up on missed work, or to ask for help from home if they are having difficulty with an assignment. Edmodo makes me easily accessible to my students outside of the classroom and allows me to give them practice completing tests and assignments online, where they can view their progress in real time! Edmodo has allowed me to be responsive to my students in real time as well. It is a great tool!

Tracy Feighery, Teacher/Technology Director
Winslow Township High School, Atco, New Jersey

• • •

Although there is currently limited research about the flipped classroom's efficacy, anecdotally students, teachers, and parents rave about its benefits. One area where the data appear strong is that for students needing additional help and remedial students, the benefits are profound—these students are able to "pause and rewind" their teachers until they "get it" (Bergmann & Sams, 2012). So, how can Edmodo help?

Implementing Your Flipped Classroom with Edmodo

Edmodo offers a wonderful way to pinpoint material to add to your flipped classroom. The Spotlight tool gives a great way to identify well-tested, popular content that other educators are successfully using. It also provides an opportunity to network much more precisely with teachers who have similar interests, or even find teachers who are teaching the same unit at the same moment! And, it offers a convenient way for you to share your flipped content to benefit even more classes than your own.

The reasons Bergmann and Sams suggest for flipping a classroom are closely aligned with the many benefits of Edmodo we outlined in Chapter 1: increased student empowerment, greater classroom organization and efficiency, better communication, and even greater personalization and differentiation through the use of a safe, private, "collaboratory" space in which students and teachers share ideas. Here is how Edmodo specifically connects with the advantages of the flipped classroom:

1. **Speaks the Language of the Digital Native.** The format of Edmodo mirrors much of the social network environment students are well aware of. This is especially true if you gamify your class.

2. **Allows You to Pause and Rewind the Teacher.** Struggling students have instant access to teacher-created content and can review it as needed. The teacher also has a convenient preorganized repository of work for future classes

3. **Increases Student-Teacher Interaction.** Edmodo offers a focused way to provide direct feedback to students and an efficient way for students to contact the teacher. It is also an effective way to communicate daily objectives, perhaps before the students even set foot in your classroom. To serve students, you need to know how they are feeling at any given moment and, as we

discussed, class polls can go a long way toward this. Students can also be invited to begin articulating exactly what they need for those face-to-face sessions.

4. **Increases Relationship Building.** Edmodo helps create a forum that gives voice to all students, even those who may be less inclined to speak in physical class discussions.

5. **Increases Student-Student Interaction.** Edmodo allows students to leverage their existing social network savvy, sharing relevant content and providing feedback on each other's work, in and out of the classroom. Students are increasingly experts in peer-to-peer tutoring (ask them how they learned about Minecraft or ComputerCraft mods on YouTube). Edmodo offers them a focused and secure forum to share knowledge and relevant skills.

6. **Facilitates Authentic Differentiation.** Edmodo offers a convenient way to offer unique learning paths to students, whether by large group, small group, or direct access to folder content, which can meet the wide variety of student needs in your classroom. (Don't forget to add a splash of gamified elements for fun!)

7. **Supports Classroom Management.** In addition to providing a source of focus for a class, Edmodo also helps mitigate a lot of classroom management issues. It gives you a place to streamline and add efficiency to your classroom practice, from grading to continual class communication to organizing content. (Use of the gamifying Class Dojo app offers one way for teachers to address behavioral issues; there is a similar free Edmodo app from Sokikom called The Class Management tool.)

8. **Supports Parent Communication.** Edmodo parent accounts, in conjunction with active use of the Planner, provide a great way to give parents a bird's-eye view of the class activities and their own child's involvement. Even when children change schools, or move from one level to the next (elementary to middle school), if the new school is using Edmodo, the parent still automatically receives notifications whenever a student is sent an assignment.

9. **Helps Make Class Transparent.** Edmodo helps give you a way to clearly articulate your class activity to parents, administrators, or other colleagues with

whom you would like to share specific or general ideas about your class. For example, if an administrator or teacher asks, "How are you gamifying your literature circles?" you can respond by inviting them to join the group and experience it in real time.

10. **Assists with Absent Students or Teachers.** This was the original reason we explored Edmodo. In an international school setting, we were often faced with school closures or students absent for extended periods of time. Edmodo is a great way for a student to still be involved, even when they are not physically present.

11. **Allows Students to Move at Their Own Pace.** If you have different levels (perhaps gamified) that you are acknowledging with badges, students can easily move at their own pace through predefined activities or "missions," allowing you to better tailor your content to their unique ability.

Edmodo is a versatile tool that supports and extends a wide variety of teaching and learning practices. We are extremely fortunate as educators to have these tools conveniently at our disposal. As we will see in the next chapter, you can also use Edmodo to efficiently document, assess, and evaluate progress toward your standards and benchmarks in your learning community.

Chapter 6

Edmodo and Assessment

*N*ow that we have considered some of the ways Edmodo can complement, enrich, and organize your existing classroom practice, we turn to some of the ways in which you can assess how effective all this is in your learning community. In this chapter, we look at assessment strategies that give you organized data as well as allow you to check in with the affective pulse of your class.

Home and Independent Activities

The Planner feature offers an efficient way to communicate home learning opportunities to the learners in your environment. A good practice each day is to place a line about whatever the activity was in that session and then a brief "INTERNET" listing homework. This, of course, clearly communicates to everyone in your learning community what's happening in your learning family. Another benefit: because the Planner (or calendar) feature integrates all of the groups to which a student belongs, the student needs to check only one place for all daily homework and upcoming projects and deadlines.

"I love doing homework!"

One of my students, who didn't like to do homework, kept asking, "Are you going to put the homework in Edmodo?"

Puzzled, I asked him why.

He replied, "I love doing homework in the computer!"

He never missed an assignment again. … Well, at least the ones he could do in Edmodo.

Mrs. Cisneros, Teacher
Miami-Dade

• • •

"Hacking" Classroom Assignments

Edmodo's Assignments feature provides the classroom teacher with an effective and efficient way to keep track of who has turned in what and when. Assignments can be graded inside of Edmodo, but they don't have to be. You can "hack" the grading system to make it simply a place to see whether things are turned in. A convenient way to do this: instead of entering a numerical score (8/10), in the boxes, simply put O/K. This doesn't affect the students' scores, but it lets you (and them) know that work is turned in and recognized. Then, as desired, you can provide much greater levels of detail and feedback, including giving a generally affective response through the custom emoticons and assignment comments. If you really want to make all of your assessment feedback completely paperless and "emotify" it, you can even mark up student documents using the annotation feature and send them back to students for possible revisions. The O/K score could now change to a numerical one, if you like. Although many educators use other grading systems that may be standard at their school, this is definitely a viable option for anyone wanting to both digitize grades as well as enter them more automatically. Remember, quizzes and other assignments that have been scored can go automatically into your grade book.

• • •

A Social Network for Us

My students use Edmodo to ask and answer questions, review for tests, and even to discuss assignments in other classes that don't use Edmodo! They love the review quizzes I post before tests, asking to take them over and over again (not for a grade but just to review).

Vanita Vance, Teacher
College Station High School, College Station, Texas

• • •

Quizzes

For busy teachers, creating quizzes in Edmodo offers an opportunity to continually come back to the quiz content, year after year, if relevant. Set it up once and there you go. Although a multitude of quiz-making programs can give you the benefits of not grading quizzes manually, doing it in Edmodo immediately integrates the scores into your grade book. Once created, quizzes can then be brought back, assigned to other classes, and used over and again. If you are giving quizzes in an environment where kids will be sitting close together and might have wandering eyes, the quizzes can be set to randomize questions so that no two students are ever likely to have the same question at the same time. You can also decide whether or not you want students to be able to review correct/incorrect answers and see their score immediately at the end of the quiz, or wait until you have reviewed them and save the sharing with the students for later. You can also choose whether or not a quiz will go into the grade book.

Quick and Easy Assessment

Edmodo provides a quick and easy way for students to submit digital work. As a Technology teacher, my students create all of their work on the computer and I am able to collect work easily and grade it in the same place. Students are able to see their grades as soon as the assignment is graded.

Kelly Vazquez, Technology Teacher
Fairfield Township School, Bridgeton, New Jersey

● ● ●

Tracking Progress

The grade book is accessed through the Progress icon in Edmodo. It has two main areas: grades and badges.

Figure 6.1 • Progress, aka the Edmodo grade book

Grades

In the Grades area (again, these can be instantly connected with assignments and quizzes), you can also add non-Edmodo grades and use this as your main grade book. Simply click on the New Grade button to add grades from another source. If you are using another program for grading, you can export data from the Edmodo grade book as a CSV file.

Badges

The Badges area offers you a quick overview of achievements and levels, which you can then easily document in the grade book where necessary, such as with an "Approaches to Learning" or Participation grade. Many apps will also automatically provide assessment data for your Progress grade book and badges.

Snapshot

Snapshot is a free embedded app that offers teachers an easy way to track class and student progress through Common Core and other standards. It automatically offers mini-assessments of pre-created standards-based questions that can then be instantly sent to any class/group stream. It also offers robust analytical data for teachers in the form of Snapshot reports.

Snapshot can be accessed through the Snapshot icon button or on the main post toolbar.

Beyond the Grade Book: Using Polls to Gauge Student Experience

Another way you can use Edmodo to assess your students is through polls. As a formative assessment, without grading, you can use polls to indicate a general class reaction. Did most students think this test was easy? Horrible? By asking and answering the poll, students self-evaluate their experience and are empowered to help shape the future of their classroom. In turn, teachers gain further information about the assessment they have just administered. If desired, students can make their feedback to the teacher even more specific by adding comments to the poll as they take it.

Now that we have considered ways you can track progress and performance, let's move on to consider how we can supercharge our own practices through creating professional learning networks in Edmodo.

Chapter 7

Building Your Professional Learning Network Using Edmodo

Now that you have transformed your classroom into a well-oiled learning machine, organizing resources and data (with a sprinkling of exploration into various other learning methods), it is time to take yourself to the next level. Tap into the sea of shared resources that Edmodo's professional networks can offer. Create a professional learning community that will enrich, expand, and support your journey. In addition to being a knowledge bank for you, it will give you a chance to mentor others and play Yoda as you share your limitless wisdom and knowledge.

One powerful element of Edmodo, beyond what it allows you to do in your own classroom, is the way in which it lets you network with other educators as well as teaching and learning resources. In this chapter, we discuss ways to leverage Edmodo for professional networking. Here, we consider effective ways to use the teacher connections, teacher-created groups, and educational communities available on Edmodo.

A Global Idea

I highly recommend any school district get on board. Teachers from other parts of the world share ideas and work, collaborate on projects that span the globe, and help each other become better teachers through the sharing of their own ideas and work.

Jo Stone, Teacher
Johnson Middle School, Bradenton, Florida

• • •

Finding and Creating Relevant Edmodo Groups

Think of your school now. Perhaps you want to start a reading group to share resources. If you are lucky, you might have a handful of interested participants at your school. Doing the same thing on Edmodo allows you to create a potential network that draws from a pool of perhaps millions, certainly more than could fit in your staff room.

Within Edmodo groups and communities, lists of teacher groups circulate informally. To find the latest one, search within Edmodo communities. There are Google docs that list dozens of available groups, such as "21st Century Administrators," groups on STEM, and groups for teachers interested in flipping and gamifying their classrooms, as well as groups about particular educational theories or particular authors. (I hear there's a great group called CodeMakers for those interested in teaching programming—*shameless plug for Raphael's own teacher group.*) You can find a group for almost any subject, and if by chance you don't find one on your particular topic, take 30 seconds and create one!

Exciting Edmodo Teacher Groups!

There are many active groups in existence on Edmodo. Here is a list of some of the major ones featured at **EdmodoCon** 2014 and their request to join codes.

Group Name	Group Join URL
So You Think You Know Your Students? Using Videos, Polls, and Reflective Response to Inform Instruction	http://edmo.do/j/w7jzvd
Edmodo That! Unique Ways to Connect and Learn	http://edmo.do/j/qzzabm
Redefining Learning with Limited Tech	http://edmo.do/j/qqrsd7
From Tech Illiterate to Tech Savvy: How to Foster Non-Cognitive Skills in Edmodo	http://edmo.do/j/jzj6dr
"Leveling Up" Student Writing With Badges	http://edmo.do/j/mncruf
Moving Beyond the Classroom Walls: Connecting Globally Through Storytelling	http://edmo.do/j/4h65wf
Solving D3: Data-Driven, Differentiated Instruction	http://edmo.do/j/xc2nq2
Creating a Diverse, College- and Career-Ready Tech Culture	http://edmo.do/j/p2d3rn
Building and Spreading the Edmodo Wildfire	http://edmo.do/j/rzdwqc
KEYNOTE: Shining a Spotlight on Our Schools: Making Students the Star of the Show	http://edmo.do/j/dcrwqv

Creating a Professional Group

It is easy to create a professional teacher group. You do it the same way you create them for students, except that here, instead of circulating the join code, you would circulate a request to join link, which allows you to moderate who joins your group. Then, to gather group members, all you do is announce it in relevant groups and communities and request to have it added to a circulating master list.

Steps to Create a Teacher Group

1. Click the + sign next to groups.

2. Answer the questions about the basics of your group (name, expected group size if you have one, grade level, subject area)

3. The group code for your new group is now listed. Circulate it privately to anyone you want. Again, it is generally considered bad form to put it into any public place.

4. Use the join URL link next to the group code, and post that anywhere.

5. Approve requests when you receive notifications that people want to join your group.

6. Your group is off and running!

• • •

Tip: Share Using Other Social Media, Too

You can share the request to join URL on any social media. If responding teachers do not yet have an Edmodo account, they'll be prompted to create one.

• • •

Teacher Connections

As you navigate through groups and communities, if someone shares posts and information that lead you to sense a kindred professional spirit, you can request a teacher connection with them. A criterion that some people use to evaluate potential connections is their sharing score. Under the teacher's name and location information, Edmodo gives each teacher points for the number of resources shared that have been added to the libraries of others. See Figure 7.1 for an example. A person with a very high sharing score has proven to be a valuable contributor to professional communities.

Figure 7.1 • Finding and creating a teacher connection

Making a Teacher Connection in Five Easy Steps

1. Click on the name of a person you are interested in connecting with professionally.

2. Check out their profile and possibly mutual connections.

3. Click on the "Add a Connection" button next to their image.

4. Wait for that person to accept your connection.

5. Keep an eye on your own notifications for connection requests from others.

• • •

Another way to identify prospective teacher connections is with the Spotlight feature we have previously discussed. When the Spotlight feature lets you know that another teacher is working on the same unit you are, that may be an ideal time to make connections and share resources.

Leveraging Communities

When we move from groups to talk about communities, we move up exponentially in terms of group member size. A teacher group may have tens and in rare cases hundreds of members, but communities often have thousands, sometimes tens of thousands of members. This is due in large part to the greater breadth of a community. Instead of focusing on a more narrow, specific interest, communities are generally formed around a wider topic.

Communities are preset groups that are organized by particular subjects (Science, Math, Creative Arts, Professional Development, etc.). Using them, you can post a question about an area you are interested in to see if a group already exists. If you are interested in it, chances are others will be, too. (Build it and they will come.)

Digital Support

When talking teacher to teacher, we can all empathize and be supportive of one another. Sometimes I just use Edmodo as a pick-me-up at the end of a long day, because I always get refreshed reading the excitement in other teacher's e-voices!

Joelle Dulaney, Middle School Teacher
Richards HS/ISD, Richards, Texas

• • •

More generally, communities are great one-stop shopping and idea share points for teachers with broad shared interests. In addition to major subject area communities, many educational companies and publishers also have communities. For example, there is a vibrant Khan Academy community. Many of the publishers you will find in communities are integrated into Edmodo through the app store as well, and their communities also act as de facto support forums for the use of those applications. Of course there are also valuable places for teachers to share how they are using specific commercial resources as well as a place to ask and answer each other's questions.

Professional Development and Edmodo

Although there is a professional development community that teachers can tap into and follow, a teacher may be well served by networking into the plethora of groups and communities that might be more specific to their individual interests. It is not uncommon to find new *and* experienced teachers asking for something as small as a lesson idea or even as big as a request for an entire curriculum. They are often amazed at the generosity of their fellow teachers' responses.

In addition to all of these available resources and networks, Edmodo can also be leveraged to offer organized professional development to your own fellow teachers or staff. Drawing from the various resources and placing relevant posts and links into a series of shared teacher folders, a staff could easily develop their own powerful, customized professional development network.

Finding and Sharing Resources

I am a school librarian and staff developer so it helps me to find resources for my colleagues. I use Edmodo in my library to co-teach virtually. Using Edmodo I am able to teach information literacy skills to students even if they aren't in the library. By co-teaching I am able to support teachers as they help their students conduct research projects. The teachers take care of the content, while I focus on the research process.

Kristina Holzweiss, Teacher, Staff Developer
Bay Shore Middle School

• • •

Chapter 8

Making Connections with Edmodo

At the heart of the ISTE Standards for Administrators, Students, Teachers, and Coaches is the underlying importance of connection: our connection with creativity and critical thinking, our connection to our own literacy in a digital space, and more broadly, our connections with others. In the digital age, we increasingly *are* our connections.

A connection by definition is something that joins two or more things together. In this final chapter we consider all the links that make the chain the strongest it can be so that we can serve each other in the most efficient and robust ways.

Connecting with Parents

As long-time educators, we really did not see how mysterious classroom life could be to a parent until we were parents ourselves and wondered, "What is happening in the classroom?" Even the most well-intentioned teacher devoted to creating the best possible learning community can be overwhelmed by the additional challenge of attempting to accurately and sufficiently communicate class life to the extended parent community. This is another place where Edmodo can be your new best friend. It allows you to give parents a view of classroom activity, a view that you as a teacher control completely.

Resource for Students and Parents

I present the Planner portion to both parents and students in conferences and in class to assist students with time management and mapping out projects and weekly study. This is a fantastic resource for students and parents!

Tawny Callaghan, Teacher
Marblehead Veterans Middle School, Marblehead, Virginia

• • •

The two main ways we suggest communicating with parents are: (1) sending occasional posts directly to them (once they have signed up for parent accounts), posts that include photos or videos of class happenings; and (2) adding quick daily entries on the class calendar/planner, which at a glance allows parents to see what's been done and what extensions or homework you have made available.

Make It Public

In addition, your main Edmodo stream can also be leveraged as a kind of class blog to the parents. Although student activity is always private (parents can only see posts by you and their own child), Edmodo offers teachers the ability to make a public version of your private group page. With any post in that stream, you can decide after the fact whether you would like it to be public or not. This gives you the opportunity to make public selected elements of class activity that you feel are relevant to give parents, or anyone else in your learning community, a sense of class activity. This is useful in that none of those viewing it even have to have Edmodo accounts. You simply circulate the public URL to them and they can view it on their web browser or from their mobile device. They can even subscribe to its RSS Feed.

With Edmodo it is surprisingly easy to keep the parent link a strong one. It helps keep parents active in the support of student achievement, while connecting home and school as never before.

Ways Parents Can Take Advantage of Edmodo

This list can be used as part of your introduction to Edmodo as you are bringing parents on board.

1. Peek into your child's progress, their latest scores, and see if assignments were turned in or not.

2. Give your child a pat on the back for any badges they have received for their achievements.

3. Get a sense of your child's participation in their digital community. (Remember, for privacy reason, parents can only see their own child's posts.)

4. Check out the cool videos and pictures teachers send out to their class parent groups to give parents a flavor of class life.

5. Check in to see when your child's assignments and homework are due.

6. Turn on notifications, and be notified by email whenever a new assignment is given to your child.

● ● ●

Connecting with Other Teachers

In the previous chapters, we spoke at length of ways you can take advantage of the incredible opportunities offered by other teachers. For your local, immediate school site, Edmodo can also be a valuable way to connect and communicate. For instance, for those teaching middle school and above especially, diligent use of the Planner can help all of the extended learning community have a sense of student workload. This can be valuable in ensuring that assessments and tests are spread out so that all tests are not given on the same day, and the homework load is balanced and as humane as possible.

Also, for true collegiality, teachers need to know about each other's practice. Some research suggests that teachers' positive relationships with each other may be one of the most important ways to encourage student success. As the Stanford Social Innovation Review reported, "Teacher social capital was a significant predictor of student achievement gains above and beyond teacher experience or ability in the classroom" (Strauss, 2014). Even though teacher schedules often make it difficult to visit a colleague's classroom, with Edmodo it is now possible. Joining each other's class Edmodo groups can help give vital insight into each other's daily practice, helping us learn with and from each other. This connection can be a small but important part in helping us create truly collegial work environments.

Connecting Classes with Experts and the Greater Community

A school is only as strong as its networks. Edmodo can be a focused and important way of nurturing immediate and extended connections that are crucial to our children's success. These networks encompass the local and the global: everything from introducing your students to professionals in their immediate community who may be able to answer questions about future paths and become a valuable pool of potential internships, mentors, and supporters of our schools, to connecting them with faraway experts, such as scientists from NASA.

Using all these professional networks can help you identify both resources and experts to infuse and enrich your content. Whether you find them through network connection in Edmodo's professional development communities and groups or elsewhere, inviting an expert from any field to be a guest in your class is both easy and valuable. Invite them to join as a teacher and bring them into one of your groups to correspond with them. For example, if your class is meeting with a scientist via Skype, create an Edmodo group that can serve as a **backchannel** (a stream to host concurrent questions and comments during a Skype or other event). To keep all the content from an event in one place and for privacy, we suggest creating a separate group for the event and the "guest lecturer" or visitor.

Making Connections for School Communities

Many schools also put a great deal of effort into leveraging social media to make connections for their school community. Edmodo is one of the only tools that, in a safe way, allows students to participate more immediately in these charged networks. This allows our schools to make a series of interactions, from the micro to the macro. The class community and collective skillset builds as students share their knowledge in one shared space. For example, during their research on space exploration leading up to a videoconference via Skype or Google Hangout with a robotics professor and NASA engineer, students share videos and articles and articulate their opinions in writing that matters—writing that has an immediate, real audience: each other. Their thoughts and ongoing research become part of an organic, ongoing conversation.

Using guided prompts, and gently steering students toward complementary resources, teachers build community by guiding students' flow of ideas, pushing out alerts and events to students, and soliciting their reactions to ongoing conversations. Teachers also "invite the world in," having the chance to welcome other teachers or experts into the conversation. Before the event, the expert can post some recent video of robotics and a relevant article to build even more enthusiasm. All of this gives the students the chance to see and experience the connection between the students' own immediate community's interconnected ideas and those of the larger world.

Using all these means of connecting with the immediate and extended community is essential to the ongoing health and vitality of our systems of learning and teaching. The intersection of these immediate and extended communities in which the students feel themselves active and vital parts—digital scholars actively pursuing ideas and solving problems together—may be Edmodo's most important lesson.

Conclusion

The right tool, at the right time, in the right hands, can truly work magic. As a tool, this is surely Edmodo's time. More importantly, as educators, it is our time. We are truly fortunate to have access to it and all the other powerful tools Edmodo helps us organize and use in our practices.

In this book, we have considered together how Edmodo can be an important part of connecting all of us in meaningful ways, of leveraging our existing tools to build cooperative learning communities—to encourage purposeful connections between students in our classrooms, between schools and their communities, and between us as teachers and administrators—and perhaps even encouraging a greater sense of connection between all of us globally.

We have looked at how Edmodo can help us inspire our students to experience their own digital *superpowers* in focused, organized ways. This environment allows students to practice these new powers responsibly, in a safe space, while learning both with and from each other. In the process, of course, students develop the essential digital age learning skills and digital citizenship practices necessary to create smart digital footprints for the rest of their coming journeys.

Along the way, we have also looked at how Edmodo offers an exciting space for us as teachers to support our instruction and assessment, as well as to experiment with methodologies and teaching and learning systems, from project-based learning, to the 1:1 program, to mobile devices and gamification. We have looked at how Edmodo can be a powerful part of expanding and supporting our professional practice, an important means of inspiring and being inspired by each other, perhaps making our schools better places in the process.

Collaborating, asking questions, and sharing ideas in the myriad communities and groups that make up Edmodo, it is easy to begin to believe that there is no problem too big to be solved together. Just about anything seems possible when each of us takes turns sharing what we know and asking for what we need. Sharing curriculum, tips, and questions and working miracles for—and with—each other, we increasingly believe that, given the right tools, there's nothing we cannot do.

Of course, when we as educators participate in and practice this kind of meaningful, lived collaboration, we are modeling the very digital citizenship and lifelong learning we hope to inspire and engender in our students.

We hope the information we have shared in this book helps encourage you to further develop your own practice and to share your discoveries, building your own interconnected communities along the way, as you swim in the digital waters of the largest pool of connected teachers in human history. In this way, each discovery on our adventures becomes our collective discovery—each of our successes a shared success. And each of our challenges is lightened.

Thank you for adding this book to your toolkit. We can't wait to see what all of us, working together, create. Together, with the ideas and tools in our hands, anything is possible.

Now, it's your turn.

What will you do next?

Appendix A
Glossary

The following terms are defined here as they specifically relate to their use in Edmodo.

app launcher. The button on the homepage that brings up the apps associated with a group(s).

assignment. A posting made by the teacher that is an activity to be completed by students by a particular day.

avatar. An image associated with a user's profile.

backchannel. An electronic forum in which participants share ideas and ask questions all related to a simultaneous live event, such as a lecture, class, or videoconference.

Backpack. A "digital locker" within Edmodo in which students can save and store any of their files and media; can be thought of as a virtual USB drive for students. *This is the student equivalent of the teacher's Library.*

badges. Visual awards (icon or image) added to a student's or teacher's profile based on specific achievements or accomplishments.

blended learning. Sometimes referred to as hybrid learning, in which instruction is done both face-to-face and online.

class management systems. Electronic platforms that allow for the management of tasks commonly associated with the classroom, such as grading, tracking student records; such systems often provide students opportunities for online activity.

code of conduct. An agreed-upon set of guidelines for what is acceptable in a particular environment.

Communities. Large preexisting groups organized by a shared major subject (such as math or science), topic area (such as professional development), or a particular publisher (such as Khan Academy or ISTE).

differentiation. Instruction that is customized to the individual learning needs of a particular learner.

digital citizenship. The series of concerns and issues surrounding the rights and responsibilities of a digital environment.

digital footprint. The digital "tracks" the activities of a user leaves behind from their online activity. This can include both data collected about users without their knowledge such as cookies, or users' public activity such as blog posts or social network activity.

digital learning. The use of electronic media, especially the internet, for learning.

Easter eggs. A convention of digital games in which nonessential information is placed in the game environment for chance discovery by experienced users.

EdmodoCon. The free, high-profile conference hosted online by Edmodo with speakers highlighting best practices and ideas for taking your Edmodo practice further.

educational social network. A social network optimized for educational users.

embed. Placing content directly into a website so that it appears automatically when a user visits that site (as opposed to offering a hyperlink that leads to another site).

filters. A feature of Edmodo that allows teachers or students to quickly drill down to a particular type of content—for example, to view only posts made by the teacher, only assignments, and so on.

flipped classroom. Model of instruction in which content instruction is done independently, generally out of the classroom in an online format through online resources, especially prerecorded teacher lecture material, and face-to-face class time is used for whole-group clarification and cooperative activity.

folders. Organized places for teachers to place files and library content. The teacher can assign access to the folder to any desired groups.

gamification. Using the structures and mechanics of games (i.e., levels, narrative, missions, etc.) to generate student interest and motivate students to acquire desired learning outcomes in both skills and content.

groups. Teacher-created grouping of students and/or teachers for a particular class, activity, or interest area.

HTML. Hypertext Markup Language, the standard coding language used to format web pages.

Library. Digital storage space that Edmodo provides teachers in which they can save content, particularly media found on Edmodo, and easily add to post or share with other users. *This is the teacher equivalent of the student Backpack.*

Likes. Feature that allows students to indicate that they "Like" a particular posting.

mission. Overarching narrative or goal within a game or gamified environment.

moderated. Setting that requires teacher to approve each post before it will appear in the stream (as opposed to the posts appearing automatically). *Not to be confused with a student-moderated group in which a student leader helps guide other students in responses to prompts.*

notifications. Notices a user receives when relevant content has been posted, such as direct responses to questions, new assignments, alerts, or teacher connection and group approval requests.

Planner. Feature that allows users to track upcoming assignments and add their own events and tasks.

professional learning community. A network of teachers and other professionals sharing ideas and resources to better their practices around a particular topic; also called professional learning networks.

professional learning network. See professional learning community.

Progress. The Edmodo grade book. Here, teachers can view and update student grades and badges. For students, this is where they would view their own individual progress.

project-based learning. Model of instruction organized around creating meaningful learning experiences, often collaborative projects for students, associated with authentic assessment.

read-only mode. Setting that allows teachers to have an individual student or class only be able to view others' postings to a group stream, as opposed to a regular student account that has full posting rights.

RSS feed. Short for Really Simple Syndication feed. Web content to which a user can subscribe a group to so that new content is automatically received on the group stream as it is posted.

simulation. Extended role-playing or imaginary activity in which all participants assume particular roles in a stated narrative or environment.

Snapshot. Assessment tool within Edmodo that allows teachers to instantly generate simple formative assessments aligned with Common Core.

social bookmarking. Social media tools that allow users to tag and direct other users to publicly available internet content.

social network. Digital network that allows users to communicate and share content with each other online.

Spotlight. Feature of Edmodo that allows users to identify and share frequently used resources for any particular subject or topic area.

stream. The main body of an Edmodo homepage on which all posted content appears.

student response systems. Physical or digital systems that allow students to instantly log their responses or answers, such as clickers.

subdomain. A customized URL for a school district. For example, GreaterLearningUnified.edmodo.com

virtual classroom. Model of instruction in which elements of a traditional classroom are emulated in a digital form.

web editors. Applications that allow one to create web pages.

Appendix B
ISTE Standards

ISTE Standards for Students (ISTE Standards·S)

All K–12 students should be prepared to meet the following standards and performance indicators.

1. **Creativity and Innovation**

   Students demonstrate creative thinking, construct knowledge, and develop innovative products and processes using technology. Students:

   a. apply existing knowledge to generate new ideas, products, or processes

   b. create original works as a means of personal or group expression

   c. use models and simulations to explore complex systems and issues

   d. identify trends and forecast possibilities

2. **Communication and Collaboration**

   Students use digital media and environments to communicate and work collaboratively, including at a distance, to support individual learning and contribute to the learning of others. Students:

   a. interact, collaborate, and publish with peers, experts, or others employing a variety of digital environments and media

   b. communicate information and ideas effectively to multiple audiences using a variety of media and formats

   c. develop cultural understanding and global awareness by engaging with learners of other cultures

   d. contribute to project teams to produce original works or solve problems

3. **Research and Information Fluency**

Students apply digital tools to gather, evaluate, and use information. Students:

    a. plan strategies to guide inquiry

    b. locate, organize, analyze, evaluate, synthesize, and ethically use information from a variety of sources and media

    c. evaluate and select information sources and digital tools based on the appropriateness to specific tasks

    d. process data and report results

4. **Critical Thinking, Problem Solving, and Decision Making**

Students use critical-thinking skills to plan and conduct research, manage projects, solve problems, and make informed decisions using appropriate digital tools and resources. Students:

    a. identify and define authentic problems and significant questions for investigation

    b. plan and manage activities to develop a solution or complete a project

    c. collect and analyze data to identify solutions and make informed decisions

    d. use multiple processes and diverse perspectives to explore alternative solutions

5. **Digital Citizenship**

Students understand human, cultural, and societal issues related to technology and practice legal and ethical behavior. Students:

    a. advocate and practice the safe, legal, and responsible use of information and technology

    b. exhibit a positive attitude toward using technology that supports collaboration, learning, and productivity

  c.   demonstrate personal responsibility for lifelong learning

  d.   exhibit leadership for digital citizenship

6.   **Technology Operations and Concepts**

Students demonstrate a sound understanding of technology concepts, systems, and operations. Students:

  a.   understand and use technology systems

  b.   select and use applications effectively and productively

  c.   troubleshoot systems and applications

  d.   transfer current knowledge to the learning of new technologies

ISTE Standards for Teachers (ISTE Standards·T)

All classroom teachers should be prepared to meet the following standards and performance indicators.

1. **Facilitate and Inspire Student Learning and Creativity**

   Teachers use their knowledge of subject matter, teaching and learning, and technology to facilitate experiences that advance student learning, creativity, and innovation in both face-to-face and virtual environments. Teachers:

   a. promote, support, and model creative and innovative thinking and inventiveness

   b. engage students in exploring real-world issues and solving authentic problems using digital tools and resources

   c. promote student reflection using collaborative tools to reveal and clarify students' conceptual understanding and thinking, planning, and creative processes

   d. model collaborative knowledge construction by engaging in learning with students, colleagues, and others in face-to-face and virtual environments

2. **Design and Develop Digital-Age Learning Experiences and Assessments**

   Teachers design, develop, and evaluate authentic learning experiences and assessments incorporating contemporary tools and resources to maximize content learning in context and to develop the knowledge, skills, and attitudes identified in the ISTE Standards for Students. Teachers:

   a. design or adapt relevant learning experiences that incorporate digital tools and resources to promote student learning and creativity

   b. develop technology-enriched learning environments that enable all students to pursue their individual curiosities and become active participants in setting their own educational goals, managing their own learning, and assessing their own progress

    c.   customize and personalize learning activities to address students' diverse learning styles, working strategies, and abilities using digital tools and resources

    d.   provide students with multiple and varied formative and summative assessments aligned with content and technology standards and use resulting data to inform learning and teaching

3. Model Digital-Age Work and Learning

Teachers exhibit knowledge, skills, and work processes representative of an innovative professional in a global and digital society. Teachers:

    a.   demonstrate fluency in technology systems and the transfer of current knowledge to new technologies and situations

    b.   collaborate with students, peers, parents, and community members using digital tools and resources to support student success and innovation

    c.   communicate relevant information and ideas effectively to students, parents, and peers using a variety of digital-age media and formats

    d.   model and facilitate effective use of current and emerging digital tools to locate, analyze, evaluate, and use information resources to support research and learning

4. Promote and Model Digital Citizenship and Responsibility

Teachers understand local and global societal issues and responsibilities in an evolving digital culture and exhibit legal and ethical behavior in their professional practices. Teachers:

    a.   advocate, model, and teach safe, legal, and ethical use of digital information and technology, including respect for copyright, intellectual property, and the appropriate documentation of sources

    b.   address the diverse needs of all learners by using learner-centered strategies and providing equitable access to appropriate digital tools and resources

    c.   promote and model digital etiquette and responsible social interactions related to the use of technology and information

    d.   develop and model cultural understanding and global awareness by engaging with colleagues and students of other cultures using digital-age communication and collaboration tools

5. **Engage in Professional Growth and Leadership**

Teachers continuously improve their professional practice, model lifelong learning, and exhibit leadership in their school and professional community by promoting and demonstrating the effective use of digital tools and resources. Teachers:

    a.   participate in local and global learning communities to explore creative applications of technology to improve student learning

    b.   exhibit leadership by demonstrating a vision of technology infusion, participating in shared decision making and community building, and developing the leadership and technology skills of others

    c.   evaluate and reflect on current research and professional practice on a regular basis to make effective use of existing and emerging digital tools and resources in support of student learning

    d.   contribute to the effectiveness, vitality, and self-renewal of the teaching profession and of their school and community

ISTE Standards for Administrators (ISTE Standards·A)

All school administrators should be prepared to meet the following standards and performance indicators.

1. **Visionary Leadership**

   Educational Administrators inspire and lead development and implementation of a shared vision for comprehensive integration of technology to promote excellence and support transformation throughout the organization. Educational Administrators:

   a. inspire and facilitate among all stakeholders a shared vision of purposeful change that maximizes use of digital-age resources to meet and exceed learning goals, support effective instructional practice, and maximize performance of district and school leaders

   b. engage in an ongoing process to develop, implement, and communicate technology-infused strategic plans aligned with a shared vision

   c. advocate on local, state, and national levels for policies, programs, and funding to support implementation of a technology-infused vision and strategic plan

2. **Digital-Age Learning Culture**

   Educational Administrators create, promote, and sustain a dynamic, digital-age learning culture that provides a rigorous, relevant, and engaging education for all students. Educational Administrators:

   a. ensure instructional innovation focused on continuous improvement of digital-age learning

   b. model and promote the frequent and effective use of technology for learning

   c. provide learner-centered environments equipped with technology and learning resources to meet the individual, diverse needs of all learners

d. ensure effective practice in the study of technology and its infusion across the curriculum

e. promote and participate in local, national, and global learning communities that stimulate innovation, creativity, and digital-age collaboration

3. Excellence in Professional Practice

Educational Administrators promote an environment of professional learning and innovation that empowers educators to enhance student learning through the infusion of contemporary technologies and digital resources. Educational Administrators:

a. allocate time, resources, and access to ensure ongoing professional growth in technology fluency and integration

b. facilitate and participate in learning communities that stimulate, nurture, and support administrators, faculty, and staff in the study and use of technology

c. promote and model effective communication and collaboration among stakeholders using digital-age tools

d. stay abreast of educational research and emerging trends regarding effective use of technology and encourage evaluation of new technologies for their potential to improve student learning

4. Systemic Improvement

Educational Administrators provide digital-age leadership and management to continuously improve the organization through the effective use of information and technology resources. Educational Administrators:

a. lead purposeful change to maximize the achievement of learning goals through the appropriate use of technology and media-rich resources

b. collaborate to establish metrics, collect and analyze data, interpret results, and share findings to improve staff performance and student learning

c. recruit and retain highly competent personnel who use technology creatively and proficiently to advance academic and operational goals

d. establish and leverage strategic partnerships to support systemic improvement

e. establish and maintain a robust infrastructure for technology including integrated, interoperable technology systems to support management, operations, teaching, and learning

5. Digital Citizenship

Educational Administrators model and facilitate understanding of social, ethical, and legal issues and responsibilities related to an evolving digital culture. Educational Administrators:

a. ensure equitable access to appropriate digital tools and resources to meet the needs of all learners

b. promote, model, and establish policies for safe, legal, and ethical use of digital information and technology

c. promote and model responsible social interactions related to the use of technology and information

d. model and facilitate the development of a shared cultural understanding and involvement in global issues through the use of contemporary communication and collaboration tools

ISTE Standards for Coaches (ISTE Standards·C)

All technology coaches should be prepared to meet the following standards and performance indicators.

1. Visionary Leadership

Technology Coaches inspire and participate in the development and implementation of a shared vision for the comprehensive integration of technology to promote excellence and support transformational change throughout the instructional environment. Technology Coaches:

a. contribute to the development, communication, and implementation of a shared vision for the comprehensive use of technology to support a digital-age education for all students

b. contribute to the planning, development, communication, implementation, and evaluation of technology-infused strategic plans at the district and school levels

c. advocate for policies, procedures, programs, and funding strategies to support implementation of the shared vision represented in the school and district technology plans and guidelines

d. implement strategies for initiating and sustaining technology innovations and manage the change process in schools and classrooms

2. Teaching, Learning, and Assessments

Technology Coaches assist teachers in using technology effectively for assessing student learning, differentiating instruction, and providing rigorous, relevant, and engaging learning experiences for all students. Technology Coaches:

a. Coach teachers in and model design and implementation of technology enhanced learning experiences addressing content standards and student technology standards

b. Coach teachers in and model design and implementation of technology-enhanced learning experiences using a variety of research-based, learner-centered instructional strategies and assessment tools to address the diverse needs and interests of all students

c. Coach teachers in and model engagement of students in local and global interdisciplinary units in which technology helps students assume professional roles, research real-world problems, collaborate with others, and produce products that are meaningful and useful to a wide audience

d. Coach teachers in and model design and implementation of technology-enhanced learning experiences emphasizing creativity, higher-order thinking skills and processes, and mental habits of mind (e.g., critical thinking, metacognition, and self-regulation)

e. Coach teachers in and model design and implementation of technology-enhanced learning experiences using differentiation, including adjusting content, process, product, and learning environment based upon student readiness levels, learning styles, interests, and personal goals

f. Coach teachers in and model incorporation of research-based best practices in instructional design when planning technology-enhanced learning experiences

g. Coach teachers in and model effective use of technology tools and resources to continuously assess student learning and technology literacy by applying a rich variety of formative and summative assessments aligned with content and student technology standards

h. Coach teachers in and model effective use of technology tools and resources to systematically collect and analyze student achievement data, interpret results, and communicate findings to improve instructional practice and maximize student learning

3. **Digital Age Learning Environments**

    Technology coaches create and support effective digital-age learning environments to maximize the learning of all students. Technology Coaches:

    a. Model effective classroom management and collaborative learning strategies to maximize teacher and student use of digital tools and resources and access to technology-rich learning environments

    b. Maintain and manage a variety of digital tools and resources for teacher and student use in technology-rich learning environments

    c. Coach teachers in and model use of online and blended learning, digital content, and collaborative learning networks to support and extend student learning as well as expand opportunities and choices for online professional development for teachers and administrators

    d. Select, evaluate, and facilitate the use of adaptive and assistive technologies to support student learning

    e. Troubleshoot basic software, hardware, and connectivity problems common in digital learning environments

    f. Collaborate with teachers and administrators to select and evaluate digital tools and resources that enhance teaching and learning and are compatible with the school technology infrastructure

    g. Use digital communication and collaboration tools to communicate locally and globally with students, parents, peers, and the larger community

4. **Professional Development and Program Evaluation**

    Technology coaches conduct needs assessments, develop technology-related professional learning programs, and evaluate the impact on instructional practice and student learning. Technology Coaches:

    a. Conduct needs assessments to inform the content and delivery of technology-related professional learning programs that result in a positive impact on student learning

b. Design, develop, and implement technology-rich professional learning programs that model principles of adult learning and promote digital-age best practices in teaching, learning, and assessment

c. Evaluate results of professional learning programs to determine the effectiveness on deepening teacher content knowledge, improving teacher pedagogical skills, and/or increasing student learning

5. Digital Citizenship

Technology coaches model and promote digital citizenship. Technology Coaches:

a. Model and promote strategies for achieving equitable access to digital tools and resources and technology-related best practices for all students and teachers

b. Model and facilitate safe, healthy, legal, and ethical uses of digital information and technologies

c. Model and promote diversity, cultural understanding, and global awareness by using digital-age communication and collaboration tools to interact locally and globally with students, peers, parents, and the larger community

6. Content Knowledge and Professional Growth

Technology coaches demonstrate professional knowledge, skills, and dispositions in content, pedagogical, and technological areas as well as adult learning and leadership and are continuously deepening their knowledge and expertise. Technology Coaches:

a. Engage in continual learning to deepen content and pedagogical knowledge in technology integration and current and emerging technologies necessary to effectively implement the ISTE Standards·S and ISTE Standards·T

b. Engage in continuous learning to deepen professional knowledge, skills, and dispositions in organizational change and leadership, project management, and adult learning to improve professional practice

c. Regularly evaluate and reflect on their professional practice and dispositions to improve and strengthen their ability to effectively model and facilitate technology-enhanced learning experiences

Appendix C
References

About Edmodo | How we got started. (n.d.). Retrieved November 9, 2014, from http://www.edmodo.com/about/

Bergmann, J., & Sams, A. (2012). *Flip your classroom: Reach every student in every class every day.* Eugene, OR: International Society for Technology in Education.

Geron, T. (2012, July 19). Edmodo raises another $25 million for education tech. Retrieved November 9, 2014, from http://www.forbes.com/sites/tomiogeron/2012/07/19/edmodo-raises-another-25-million-for-education-tech/

Kaplan Test Prep survey finds that college admissions officers' discovery of online material damaging to applicants nearly triples in a year. (2012, October 4). Retrieved November 9, 2014, from http://press.kaptest.com/press-releases/kaplan-test-prep-survey-finds-that-college-admissions-officers-discovery-of-online-material-damaging-to-applicants-nearly-triples-in-a-year

McGonigal, J. (2010, February). Jane McGonigal: Gaming can make a better world [Video file]. Retrieved from http://www.ted.com/talks/jane_mcgonigal_gaming_can_make_a_better_world

Ribble, M. (2014, January 1). Nine Themes of Digital Citizenship. Retrieved November 9, 2014, from http://www.digitalcitizenship.net/Nine_Elements.html

Schmidt, E. (October 10, 2013). Technology as a spark for growth. Lecture conducted from Megaron Plus, Athens, Greece.

Strauss, V. (2014, October 19). The glue that really holds a school together — and that reformers ignore. Retrieved November 9, 2014, from http://www.washingtonpost.com/blogs/answer-sheet/wp/2014/10/19/the-glue-that-really-holds-a-school-together-and-that-reformers-ignore/

Index

Note: Page numbers followed by *f* indicate figures.